Pioneer Trails of the Oregon Coast

BY SAMUEL N. DICKEN

OREGON HISTORICAL SOCIETY
1971

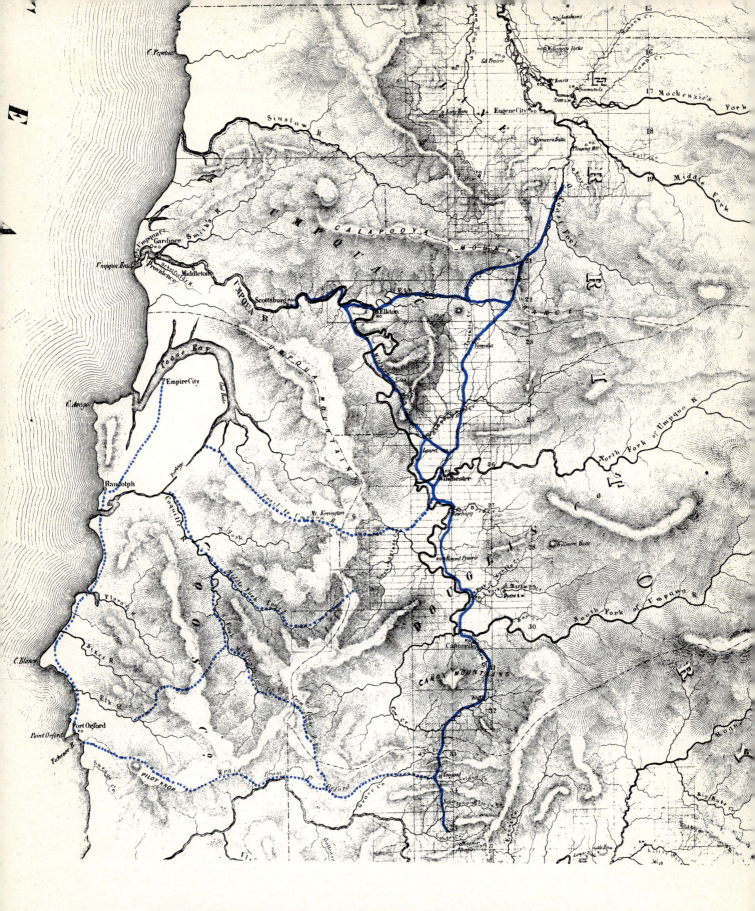

Though only one coast trail appears on the Oregon Surveyor General's 1855 map—from Port Orford to Empire City—and on to Umpqua City and Ft. Umpqua, this section of *Preston's ... Map of Oregon and Washington West of the Cascade Mountains* (by J. W. Trutch and G. W. Hyde, 1856), indicates connections from coast ports and gold bearing sands to interior mining and settled areas of southern Oregon (dotted blue lines). (OHS map file)

Preface

THIS study, aided by a grant from the Office of Scientific and Scholarly Research of the University of Oregon, deals with the historical geography of coastal pioneer trails during the period of settlement, for the most part before 1860. The Oregon Coast is presented as it was seen through the eyes of early travelers, and against the background of coastal features, climate, terrain, drainage and vegetation. Though this is a geography of a past period, it also includes relevant firsthand descriptions of coastal features, in the present tense, based on many years of field study by the writer.

I enjoyed this work. The Oregon Coast is still often wild and spectacular. Geographically, it is an experience more appreciated in recent times than it was by early entrepreneuring fur trade mariners or mineral and town site explorers who viewed its rugged contours and dangers sometimes too closely. Then it was new country, with only game and Indian trails. Readers, perhaps, may visualize how it was, compared to the ease of reaching many breath-taking scenic vistas today. It is hoped, too, that those who are aware of any visible remnants of the old trails here missed or omitted, or any errors, will report them to the author, or the Oregon Historical Society.

The publication of this original work was made possible through the Western Imprints Fund, Oregon Historical Society, and the Louis and Maud Hill Family Foundation, St. Paul, Minnesota.

SAMUEL N. DICKEN

Port Orford, Oregon, in its heyday in 1850s.
Harper's New Monthly Magazine, October 1856.

Contents

PAGE

PREFACE iii

WHY AND HOW SETTLERS CAME TO THE OREGON COAST 1

    Geography at the Time of Settlement
        Terrain
        Natural Vegetation
        Coastal Streams and Bays
        Trail Location

TRAILS OF THE NORTHERN COAST 13

    Clatsop Plains
    Cannon Beach-Nehalem Area
    Tillamook Area
    Nestucca Area

TRAILS OF THE MIDDLE OREGON COAST 37

    Siletz-Yaquina Area
    Alsea-Heceta Head Area

TRAILS OF THE SOUTHERN OREGON COAST 49

    Siuslaw-Umpqua Area
    Coos Bay-Coquille Area
    Cape Ferrelo Area
    Gold Beach-Port Orford Area
    Cape Blanco Area

FROM TRAILS TO ROADS 75

NOTES 77

Illustrations

	page		page
Yaquina Head chart, 1868	cover	Fig. 24. Aerial view, Tillamook plain	27
Coast Range, Clatsop Co.	title page	Cape Meares	28
Oregon Coast, 1856	ii	Fig. 25. Maxwell Point	29
Port Orford, 1850s	iv	Fig. 26. Cape Lookout trail	30
Fig. 1. Elk; Cape Falcon	x	Fig. 27. South of Cape Lookout	31
Fig. 2. Clatsop Plains chart	2	Fig. 28. Nestucca area trails	32
Fig. 3. Clatsop Plains photo	3	Fig. 30. Cascade Head, Salmon River	34
Fig. 4. Whalehead Cove	4	Fig. 29. Nestucca River trails	35
Figs. 5, 6. Beaches; dunes	6	Fig. 32. Siletz area trails	36
Figs. 7, 8. Marine terrace; Nehalem Bay	8	Figs. 31, 35. Crescent Beach; Cape Foulweather	38
Fig. 9. Curry Co. DLCs, trail	10-11	Figs. 33, 34. Whale Cove, Otter Rock	39
Fig. 10. Northern Coast Trail	14	Fig. 36. Yaquina area trails	40
Fig. 11. Trails, Seaside-Tillamook	16	Fig. 37. Yaquina Bay chart, 1868	41
Figs 12, 13. Tillamook Head south; trails near Seaside	17	Fig. 38. Trails, Seal Rocks-Siuslaw River	42
Fig. 14. Chart Tillamook Head	18	Fig. 40. Coast storm	43
Fig. 16. Hug Point road	20	Fig. 39. Cape Perpetua trails	44
Figs. 17, 18. Neahkahnie Mt.	21	Fig. 42. Sea Lion Point	45
Fig. 15. Tillamook Head trails	22	Fig. 41. Heceta Head	46
Fig. 20. First road, Neahkahnie Mt.	23	Fig. 43. Umpqua area trails	48
Fig. 22. Neahkahnie Mt. chart	24	Fig. 44. Army Ft. Umpqua, 1850s	50
Fig. 19. Neahkahnie Mt.—trail and road	25	Figs. 45, 46. Marshfield-Drain stage; dunes south of Umpqua	51
Fig. 23. Tillamook area trails	26	Fig. 47. Coos Bay area trails	52

	page		page
Fig. 49. Coos Bay chart, 1889	53	Fig. 55. Curry Co. natural bridges	64
Fig. 48. Boat-stage meeting, Coos Bay; Cape Arago view	54	Fig. 56. Cape Sebastian trail	65
Fig. 51. T 25 S, R 13 W (1857)	56	Fig. 57. Gold Beach and Port Orford area trails	66
Empire City, 1856	57	Fig. 58. Rogue River area chart	67
Fig. 52. Cape Arago trails	58	Figs. 59, 60. Rogue River trails; landslide	68
Fig 50. Bandon area trails	59	Fig. 61. South of Humbug Mt.	69
Marshfield-Drain stage	60	Fig. 62. North of Humbug Mt.	70
View south from Cape Blanco	61	Fig. 64. Port Orford chart, 1851	71
Fig. 53. Chetco-Cape Ferrelo trails	62	Fig. 63. Cape Blanco area trails	72
Fig. 54. Aerial view Whalehead Beach	63	Fig. 65. Cape Blanco aerial view	73
		Roosevelt Highway photos	75-76

Pioneer Trails

of the Oregon Coast

Fig. 1. Elk trails along Oregon Coast through forest and brush were large enough for a man, but not for a man on horseback. (Ore. Game Commission photo) Game trails and path are visible on photo below of Cape Falcon, Oswald West State Park area. (Ore. State Highway Division photo)

Why and How Settlers Came to the Oregon Coast

ELK made the first trails on the Oregon Coast large enough for a man to follow (Fig. 1). When man arrived, 10,000 years or more ago, he widened some of these trails and made them his own. Both elk and Indian migrated with the seasons from the shore toward the interior, but neither traveled very far along the coast. White men—miners, trappers, missionaries, settlers—when they came to the coast, found a maze of trails not very suitable to their purposes and scarcely usable for pack horses.

As a place of settlement, the Oregon Coast offered both attractions and disadvantages: there were friendly Indians, long beaches, level terraces, plenty of fish, game, timber, and water; there were also hostile Indians, difficult terrain, dense vegetation, and quicksand; rain, fog, wide streams and estuaries to cross, mud, swamps, and marshes. The choice of settlement sites and the location of trails can best be understood if it is recalled that knowledge of the area was very limited; there were few maps, few written descriptions, and word-of-mouth descriptions were often conflicting. The settlers reacted not so much to the realities of the environment as to their limited and sometimes mistaken notions of it. A few choices of farm settlement were unwise. The Clatsop Plains, for example, proved too sandy for pioneer farming (Figs. 2 and 3). This was obvious even to the inexpert eye of J. H. Frost,[1] the missionary, who lived on the Plains in 1840. The sandy nature of the soil, which made it easy to travel at any season, accentuated the drought in the dry summer.

Settlers were attracted to the Oregon Coast by the possibilities of fishing, trapping, mining, farming, and logging. Mining played an important role, particularly on the southern coast, in the early days, although the best gold deposits in the terraced gravels and the beach sands were soon exhausted. Many settlers who came to mine remained to farm. The early settlement sites chosen were, in many cases, those previously occupied by Indians, but the white settlements soon became more extensive. Most favored locations for settlements were near the outlets of the larger rivers, especially if there were good level terrace lands, but not directly on the shore.

Having reached the coast, prospective settlers often wished to travel long distances *along* the shore, so the Indian trails were modified and new trails and routes were established, more or less by trial and error, changing with the times, as new settlements were founded and old ones abandoned. Unused trails soon disappeared under the rapid growth of shrubs and trees, and only faint traces remain today. Many trails were obliterated later by the construction of roads which followed the same routes.

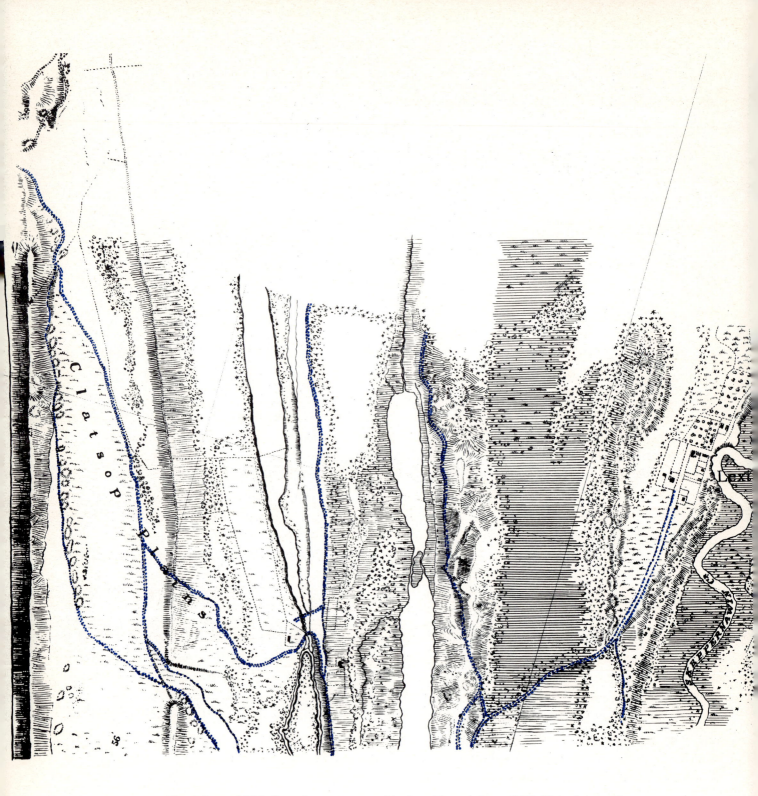

Fig. 2. Part of U.S. Coast Survey topographic chart T 1112 (793, OHS file), done 1868 by Cleveland Rockwell, and showing trails in the Clatsop Plains. Lexington, later called Skipanon or Skippernawin (near present Warrenton), marked the northern end of the main trail. Trails are marked in blue.

Fig. 3, p. 3. The Clatsop Plains, five miles north of Seaside. The main trail followed the low dune ridges near the present route of Highway 101 (which crosses from center to left north of West Lake). (Oregon State Highway photo)

By the early 1850s it was possible for a traveler to traverse the entire Oregon Coast from the Columbia River to the Winchuck River on beaches and well-used trails, touching all the important settlements on his way. There is no record of a traveler making the entire journey, but trips of 40 miles or more were common. In 1826, Chief Trader Alexander R. McLeod traveled, in two separate journeys, from the Big Nestucca River to the Rogue River.[2] In 1828, American trapper and explorer Jedediah Smith and his party traveled along the coast from the California line to the Umpqua River, a distance of approximately 150 miles, where his party was attacked by Indians.[3] One of the survivors of the Umpqua massacre, Arthur Black, found his way along the coast to Tillamook Bay, traveling an additional 150 miles.

Fig. 4. Whalehead Cove and Beach, Curry County, provided a landing for small craft in calm seas. Here the northbound traveler left the shore to take the inland ridge trail. Jedediah Smith and party camped here in 1828. (Oregon State Highway photo)

Most settlers came to the Oregon Coast by land, comparatively few by sea. Few satisfactory harbors were available in the early days, but attempts were made, some of them successful, to land in the estuaries of the large rivers and even in some of the small ones.

A survey was made of the Pacific Coast of Oregon in 1849 and 1850. In the light of the numerous wrecks in the following decade, the report was perhaps a little optimistic:

> From Cape St. George to the Toutounis, or Rogue's river, there are no special dangers. In the summer, vessels may anchor anywhere along the coast, and there are landing places south of all the rocky points. The Toutounis, or Rogue's river, has but 10 feet on the bar, is rapid, and passes between high mountains. . . .
>
> Ewing Harbor [now Port Orford] is a safe anchorage in summer. There is no surf in the landing cove.
>
> From Cape St. George to Cape Orford [now Cape Blanco], the coast is thickly inhabited by bands of wild Indians, and care is necessary not to be surprised by them.
>
> There is a reef of rocky islets off Cape Orford.[4]

Landings in the estuaries of the coastal rivers, the Nehalem, Tillamook, Yaquina, Alsea, Siuslaw, Umpqua, Coos, Coquille, Rogue, and Chetco, were usually hazardous and resulted in many wrecks. A few sheltered coves were used, Port Orford and Whalehead, for example (Fig. 4). Landings on open beaches were rare, although the first settler in the Clatsop Plains, Solomon Smith, made such a landing. Indians sometimes put to sea in their large canoes but usually for short distances and only in favorable weather and in calm seas. When settlers persuaded Indians to undertake longer coastwise voyages, the results were usually unsatisfactory and in some cases disastrous. Indians with canoes were hired to bring goods from Astoria to Tillamook in the early 1850s, but the canoes were wrecked and the cargo lost.[5] The disappointed settlers blamed the wreck on "spirits," some of which were unwisely included in the cargo. Nevertheless, efforts continued to supply the settlers by sea and to take out their produce; and sea traffic slowly increased.

The use of the inland waters was another story. Every river, estuary, and creek which would float a canoe was used in preference to pack animals or backpacking. Even small streams could be used in times of high water. In this respect the Indians showed the way and in the early days furnished the canoes and paddlers—for a price, of course.

Travel on the trails had its own hazards and uncertainties; furthermore, it was hard work. The chief problem for travelers from the Willamette Valley, or from points south on the Oregon-California Trail, was crossing the Coast Range. Tributary stream valleys on both sides of the range were followed to find low passes. The Yamhill-Nestucca route, followed by J. H. Frost in 1841, was used by travelers to Tillamook, while the Umpqua River was on the principal route to Coos Bay. Other routes were used from time to time, for there are many low passes over the Coast Range. The difficulties included dense vegetation and the lack of well-defined trails. Trails there were, made by elk and Indians—too many in fact, so that the traveler often became confused and lost. Some trails were cleared for military purposes; one such is described by Oscar Winslow Hoop:

The impracticability of supplying the troops over twenty-five miles of mountain trail did not seem insurmountable, and a road was ordered built from Kings Valley to the Siletz [Indian Reservation. Lt. Philip H.] Sheridan began the work at once. Owing to the rainy season it was only partially completed when spring came... After six months the road could be used as a fairly decent trail for pack mules, and such it remained to the end.[6]

Geography at The Time of Settlement

On the whole, the environment of the Oregon Coast was not especially favorable for either settlement or travel; the many empty areas on or near the coast today are mute testimony to this fact. Much of the coast is rugged, hilly land with steep slopes, especially near the shore, difficult for travel and affording little level land for farms or towns. In 1850 William P. McArthur in his coast survey noted: "The face of the country is too uneven to permit . . . general cultivation, still it will and must soon become a great agricultural and stock growing country."[7]

An important factor in the environment, as seen by the settlers, was the Indians themselves. Although some were hostile, most were friendly and of great assistance to the settlers, in spite of generally harsh treatment. They sold salmon to the settlers at a very low price, they supplied canoes for crossing and traveling along the rivers, and acted as guides on the trails. But the possible presence of hostile Indians in the early days undoubtedly influenced the location of trails and settlements. For example, travel on the beaches was sometimes avoided because the traveler was visible for many miles. It was preferable to go inland for a little way and fight the brush rather than to show oneself on long stretches of open beach.

The coastal Indians were divided into numerous small culture groups with distinct languages and little intercommunication.[8] Some were hostile, some friendly; in general the Indians of the northern coast were most helpful and cooperative to the settlers. By 1856 most of the hostile Indians were placed on reservations and this hazard to travel was essentially removed.

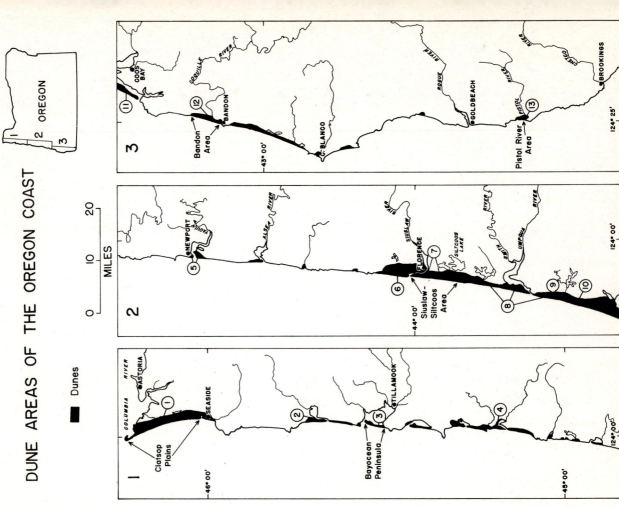

Fig. 5. Map of Oregon beaches. More than two-thirds of Oregon's 400-mile shoreline has beaches but many of them were not used by early travelers. Where there were no local names, beaches have been titled for convenience (Sacchi, Bastendorff, Houst-Enader).

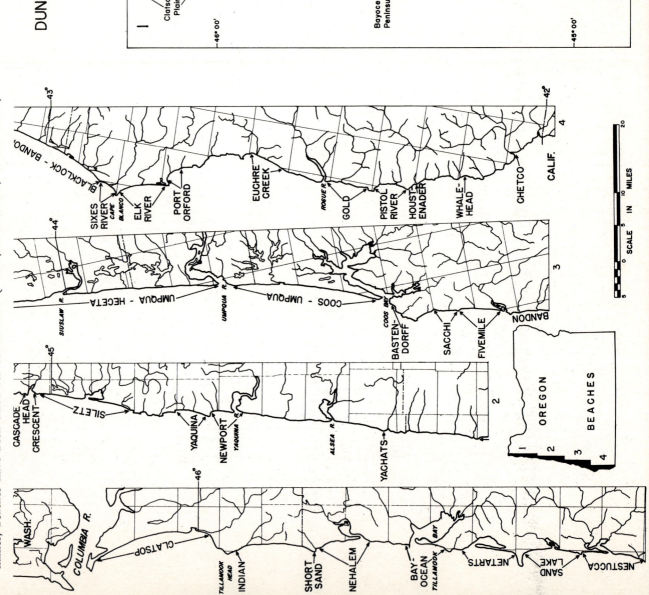

Fig. 6. Map of sand dune areas of Oregon Coast. Travelers sometimes left the beaches and traveled over the dunes in stormy weather.

DUNE AREAS OF THE OREGON COAST

The Terrain

The coastal terrain includes beaches, dunes, marshes, sea cliffs, terraces, and headlands (Fig. 5). Beaches occupy more than two-thirds of the coast but many of them are short, bordered by steep cliffs, and terminated by steep headlands, so they are of little use for travel. There is a common notion that travel on the Oregon Coast in the early days was easy because of the beaches. In some cases this was true, in others not so; at high tide and during storms the beaches, even the best ones, are unfavorable.

Good beaches afford a means of travel either on foot, with pack animals, or with vehicles. The stage coaches used the beaches extensively. At low tide the exposed beach presents a hard, smooth surface, often described by the early travelers as a "pavement." When the tide is high, however, the traveler is forced up onto the loose upper beach, which is by no means easy for travel. During storms the beaches are covered by waves and swash and are exposed to heavy winds which drive sand into the face of the traveler. Even in winter when the rains are falling, the sand blows extensively.

If beach travel is not favorable because of waves and storms, the traveler, in many places, can take to the dunes or terraces (Fig. 6). The dune adjacent to the beach, usually described as the foredune, long, narrow, somewhat hummocky, affords relatively dry footing even in wet weather. The active dunes, however, are tiresome to walk upon. In many cases the beaches are bordered on the inland side by steep sea cliffs and terminated by steep headlands, so that many beaches of fair length are not readily accessible, especially with pack animals. Jedediah Smith lost a mule south of Humbug Mountain as the party left the beach and climbed the sea cliff to the Brush Creek Trail.[9]

In many places along the Oregon Coast, marine terraces (Fig. 7) provided level land for the traveler and settler. These represent the former levels of the ocean and consist, on the surface, of deposits usually of sand, gravel, cobbles, and boulders, overlying bedrock. For these reasons they are comparatively dry and not usually muddy. Many of the settlements on the Oregon Coast are related in part, at least, to terraces, as will be seen by the individual descriptions to follow. In many places the terrace gravels contained gold and other valuable minerals and these were exploited in the early days.

The headlands offered serious obstacles to the travelers. Coming to the end of a long, smooth beach, a traveler met a steep headland, very difficult to cross, particularly with pack animals. Tillamook Head, Neahkahnie Mountain, and Cape Sebastian are good examples. Nearly all of the capes and headlands presented some difficulties to travelers.

The Natural Vegetation

Another important hazard for the traveler was the natural vegetation, although in a strict sense much of the vegetation was not natural. Before the coming of the whites the Indians had burned over the land and regrowth, dense brush or chaparral, presented a real hazard for travel, not only because of the density of the woody growth but the speed with which a trail would grow up in brush again after it was once cleared or opened.

The Indians had burned over much of the coastal areas mostly for the purpose of driving game or of making the forage more attractive for game,[10] but the whites burned even more, in order to clear land for crops and to keep the trails open. It was common practice to set fires as travelers moved along trails. Many specific accounts of burning are available, as in the Quick Family Memoirs by Flora E. Dunne.[11] The family had bought land on Lampa Creek, near the Coquille River, in 1874. They immediately set fire to old logs,

Fig. 8 (above). Early travelers usually crossed Nehalem Bay in Indian canoes, taking advantage of the north-south stretch of the river. Landings were located approximately at points A and B. Neahkahnie Mountain is at upper left.

Fig. 7 (right). At many points along the Oregon Coast marine terraces bordered by sea cliffs make up the shoreline. The narrow, steep beach is not a safe place to travel so the early trail was located at the edge of the terrace (see Fig. 20). Blacklock Point in the foreground, Floras Lake upper left, Curry County coast. (Oregon State Highway photos)

stumps, and brush; and for 15 years they kept the fires burning, whenever possible, until the land was finally cleared.

Many of the Indian trails were undoubtedly overgrown before the settlers had occasion to use them. In a few places open prairie made traveling easy and also provided forage for the pack horses. The patches of prairie tended to be along the ridge crests and many of the early trails followed such crests, which had the additional advantage of having few streams to cross. In some areas dense forest growth was found and in some of these travel was comparatively easy. In the climax forest there was little undergrowth so that the traveler and his pack animals could find their way amongst the forest trees. Undoubtedly many of the trails were chosen with this in mind, because of the difficulty of traveling through the brushy areas.

The Coastal Streams and Bays

The streams and bays of the coastal areas, ranging from small creeks to large rivers, offered more advantages for travel than disadvantages (Fig. 8). At first glance it would seem that crossing the large rivers would have been difficult for the early travelers, but this was not the case since, as previously mentioned, Indians were usually available to ferry the traveler across, swimming his horse, if he had one, behind the canoe. But Indian canoes were not always immediately available and soon enterprising white settlers built boats, took over the ferry business, and quickly "discouraged" Indian competition. These rowboats could carry a few persons with their packs and provided an easy and efficient method of transportation, not only across the streams but along them. To be sure, their line of operation was limited to the larger streams and estuaries. Many streams run parallel to the coast a short distance inland and these afforded alternate routes to those along the coast itself, either on the beach or on nearby terraces and hills. A single journey might involve travel by horseback, by boat and/or afoot.

Trail Locations

An important factor in the location of the pioneer trails was the presence of the elk and Indian trails. It is no easy matter to document the location of the Indian trails. Some of the early travelers noted the use of Indian trails but a little later travelers apparently assumed that the main trail was a white man's trail. Both Indian and pioneer tended to keep near the shore, unless the terrain became too difficult; when it did the pioneers usually climbed to higher and safer ground. In many places only one location for a trail was at all feasible.

Placer gold mines were active at various points along the southern Oregon Coast for a brief period, but they played an important part in the location and character of the trails. Placers were worked for a time, at least, at Randolph near Whisky Run south of Coos Bay, at Bandon, Port Orford (sketch on page iv), Gold Beach, and Whalehead, all in the early 1850s. Thus the early trails were oriented to these points (see map opposite Preface).

Trails also led from the coast to the mines in the interior, both on the upper reaches of the smaller coastal streams and still farther inland on the larger rivers. The greatest activity was in Josephine and Jackson counties. Supplying these mines was a serious problem. Supplies came over the Oregon-California Trail from the Willamette Valley, but also came from the coast. As pointed out previously, there was no easy route from the coast to the interior between the Coquille River and the Smith River in northern California. Nevertheless, some trails were established. A

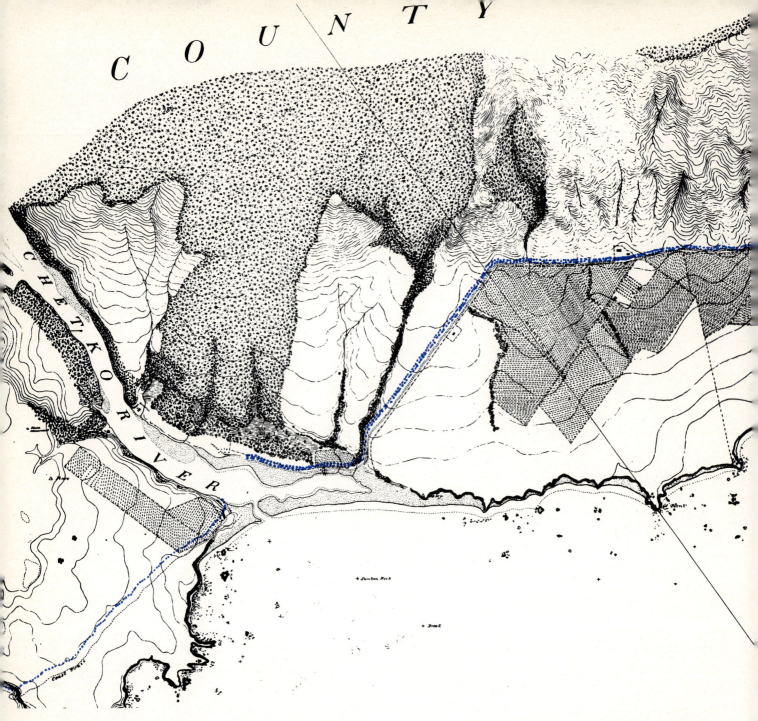

trail from Port Orford to Illahe on the Rogue River was used in the Indian wars of 1855-1856, as well as by miners. Another trail from Port Orford reached the Johnson Creek placer mines, near the South Fork of the Coquille River. Another track led over the hills east of Langlois to Myrtle Point.[12] After the Indian wars and placer mining declined, these inland trails were little used.

One of the first attempts to establish trails was by Capt. William Tichenor, who landed a party of 65 men at Port Orford in June, 1851.[13] Two parties, one on foot, the other on horses, were sent out to find a suitable pack route to the Jackson County mines. The foot party returned in a few days after becoming hopelessly lost. The horse party under William G. T'Vault also became lost in the headwaters of the South Fork of the Coquille River, abandoned their horses, and made their way back to the coast via the Coquille River; T'Vault returned via the Sixes River. Later, trails were established from Port Orford to some of

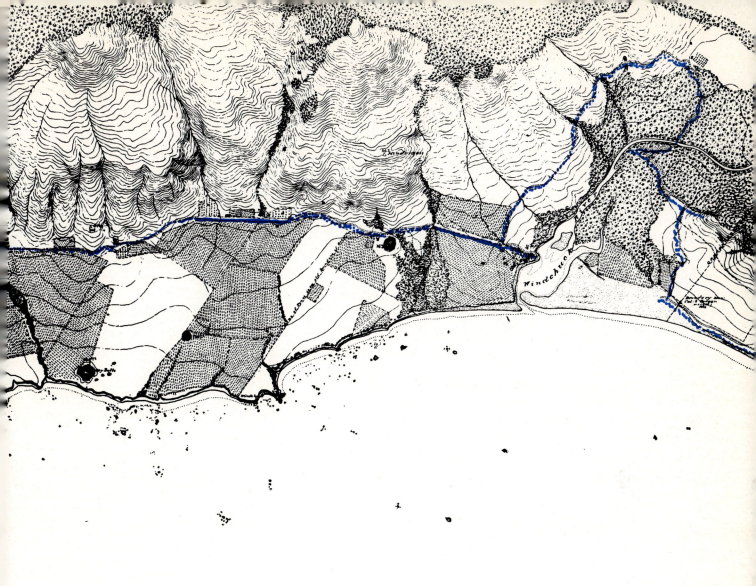

Fig. 9. A portion of U. S. Coast Survey Chart (T 1227, No. 756a, OHS), 1870, shows the location of the Coast Trail in Curry County. By that time, the trail had been relocated, in part to conform with the boundaries of the donation land claims.

the interior mining districts but were abandoned when mining ceased.

The descriptions above indicate in a general way some of the advantages and disadvantages encountered by the early settlers of the Oregon Coast. In the detailed accounts to follow attention will be given to a description of the individual areas as to terrain, vegetation, and drainage; the location and explanation of the routes of travel and settlements as seen through the eyes of the travelers, wherever possible.

During the first period of effective occupation, the principal settlements in the north were on the Clatsop Plains and around Tillamook Bay; and in the south from Umpqua Bay to the California line. Between Tillamook Bay and the Umpqua River, settlement, except for a few individuals, came later. This middle coast was considered worthless by many; furthermore, much of it was occupied by the Coast Indian Reservation and hence not open to settlement. Generally, land for settlement was easy to obtain. Before

1850 the settlers occupied land according to choice or laws of the Oregon Provisional Government; from 1850 to 1855 the donation land claim law was in effect. The location of the claims and other settlements brought about minor variations in the pioneer trails (Fig. 9). In detail the trails were constantly changing as new settlements were established or old ones abandoned.

The locations of the trails on the maps in this report are derived from a number of sources, chiefly old maps and the accounts of early travelers. The topographic charts of the U.S. Coast Survey (later called the Coast and Geodetic Survey), cited in the captions by number and date, were especially useful, although in some cases the mapped portion does not extend far enough inland to include all the trails. Copies of these maps are available in the Oregon Historical Society Library. The Land Office maps of the U.S. Surveyor General, cited in the captions by township, range, and date, were also useful. A complete set of these township maps, many of which were resurveyed from time to time, is filed on aperture cards in the Portland Office of the U.S. Bureau of Land Management, and also at OHS. Unfortunately, some of the maps and charts show no trails at all even though trails were known to exist; it is understandable, perhaps, that trails were not shown in sections where most of the travel was on the beach. In compiling the maps in this report it is intended to include only the main trails along the coast; other trails existed from time to time, but they are certainly not all included here. If any reader has additional and more specific information, the author would be grateful.

Trails of the Northern Oregon Coast

For the most part the early trails on the northern coast served two areas of settlement, the Clatsop Plains and the Tillamook Plain; a few other settlements were established at various points along the trails. Settlement began on the Clatsop Plains in 1840 and on the Tillamook Plain about ten years later. The main routes of travel to and from the Willamette Valley formed a crude circle. Astoria, Fort Vancouver, the middle Willamette Valley, the upper Yamhill River, the Nestucca River, and Tillamook were "points" on the circle. When the missionary, J. H. Frost, traveled from Clatsop Plains to the missions in the middle Willamette Valley in 1840 he went by canoe up the Columbia and Willamette rivers and returned the same way; in a later journey he traveled overland via Tillamook, the Nestucca, and the Yamhill rivers. Ten years later the Tillamook pioneer, Warren Vaughn, made the complete circle.[14] The descriptions of trails and settlements to follow are arranged by sections from north to south, corresponding to the U.S. Geological Survey quadrangles, which are used as base maps.

The Clatsop Plains

The Clatsop Plains (Fig. 10) extend from Tillamook Head (Seaside) northward to the Columbia River, and consist of long, narrow, parallel, sandy ridges with intervening lower areas, some of them marshy. A number of long, narrow lakes occur here of which Coffenbury, Smith, Cullaby, and Sunset lakes are examples. These are the result of stream courses being dammed by drifting sand. This was one of the first areas of the Oregon Coast to be settled and most of the claims were located in a long, narrow corridor about one mile from the coast. Charles Stevens described Clatsop Plains in 1854:

> The country is perhaps the most curious that you ever saw. Just take your map and find Point Adams, at the mouth of this river and run down the coast 20 or thirty miles and you will pass along the western lines of all their claims, here is a high sand ridge, and handsome beach where you can drive a horse and buggy, or a dozen of them together the whole length. About half a mile back of the ridge is another and about one fourth that distance from this is a third ridge which runs the whole length of the Plains, just as straight as the lines on this paper. These ridges are narrow on the top, hardly wide enough for two wagons to pass, and from ten to 30 feet high. Inside this third ridge are a most of their farms.[15]

At the time of settlement, the shoreline was different from the present one. This is a prograding coast—that is, the coast is being built up and advancing to the westward as the Columbia River brings large quantities of sand. At the time of settlement the shoreline was about one-eighth mile farther east at the Necanicum River on the south, about one-half mile in the middle portion of the Plain, and nearly three-fourths of a mile at Point Adams in the north. (Then there was no Clatsop Spit as we know it today. Clatsop Spit was developed partly because of the construction of

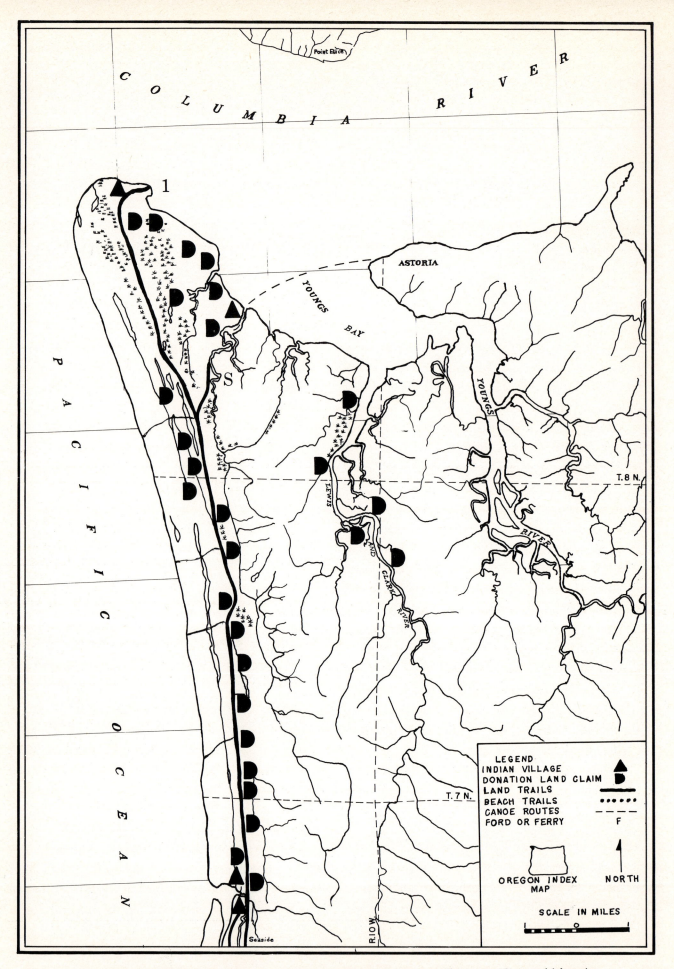

Fig. 10. The northern section of the Coast Trail. The trail began at Skipanon (S) at which point water transportation was available to Astoria. The continuation of the trail northward to Point Adams (1) was of minor importance. Side trails led to the beach and to the wooded area on the east. Base map: Astoria Quadrangle, U.S.C.E. U.S. Coast Survey charts T 1112 (1868) and T 1381 (1874), and Land Office maps T8N R10W (1856), T7N R10W (1856), and T6N R10W (1856).

the south jetty in the Columbia River.) On the Columbia River itself the shoreline was also quite different. It was low and marshy for the most part, with a number of small streams entering the river, the most significant of which was Skipanon River. To the east of the sandy ridges were the Clatsop Hills, low, rounded, and tree-covered.

Access to Clatsop Plains was mostly by way of the Columbia River; and from the south by trail. Small boats could carry the travelers or settlers across Youngs Bay and into the estuary of Skipanon River, a very short stream that would ordinarily be called a creek. Here, near the present site of Warrenton (see Fig. 2), the settlers landed and traveled overland a short distance to the Plain. The greatest difficulties for land travel were the low, swampy areas, which were flooded in the winter, and the areas of loose sand. The best route followed the long, narrow ridges but, on the whole, travel was comparatively easy, especially north and south. These ridges were old foredunes with just room enough on top for a trail or road. This route paralleled the beach about one mile inland and corresponds very closely to the present Highway 101. It was immediately west of the timbered area where most of the farmsteads were located. Here water was available everywhere in shallow wells, as well as wood from the forest. J. H. Frost, having no spade, dug the first well with an Indian canoe paddle.[16] To the north of Skipanon Landing a trail led to Point Adams with a connecting trail to the beach, but there is little evidence that the beach was used extensively for north-south travel after the dune ridge trail was established.

Settlements were developed on Clatsop Plains very rapidly in the early 1840s. There were at least 20 donation land claims in the narrow belt along the west, and there were also five or more claims on Lewis and Clark River to the east of the hilly section. Clatsop Plains was attractive to the early settlers partly because of the thin vegetation. Most of the area was grassy or covered with low shrubs, so it was by no means difficult to clear land and put it into cultivation. However, the settlers soon found that they had not selected a very good area for agriculture; the sand is too coarse, infertile, and too subject to drought in the summer when the rains are light. Often the settlers after spending a short time on Clatsop Plains moved out, many of them southward to the Tillamook area. Settlers along Lewis and Clark River were more fortunate in that the soils were developed from river flood material and bay deposits, were much more fertile, and also were not so subject to drought.

THE CANNON BEACH–NEHALEM AREA

The Cannon Beach-Nehalem Area (Fig. 11) contrasts in many ways with Clatsop Plains. Aside from that part around the lower Necanicum River at Seaside, there is very little land along the coast suitable for cultivation. Also there are several obstacles to travel along the coast, especially Tillamook Head, Cape Falcon, and Neahkahnie Mountain. Tillamook Head is a massive elevation extending out into the sea, underlain by basalt and resistant sediments. Its highest point is 1,200 feet and its western margins consist of very high and steep sea cliffs much subject to landslides. The head is dissected by short canyons, some of which are tributary to Circle Creek on the north; others run directly into the sea. On the south side of the head is the Ecola Park area (Fig. 12), underlain by shales which are especially subject to landslides. From this area small points project out into the ocean, themselves the result of former landslides. These are separated by short beaches, Indian Beach and, to the south of Chapman Point, Crescent Beach.

Captain William Clark crossed Tillamook Head in January, 1806.[17] Previously he had reached Clatsop Plains by canoe from Fort Clatsop to Skipanon Land-

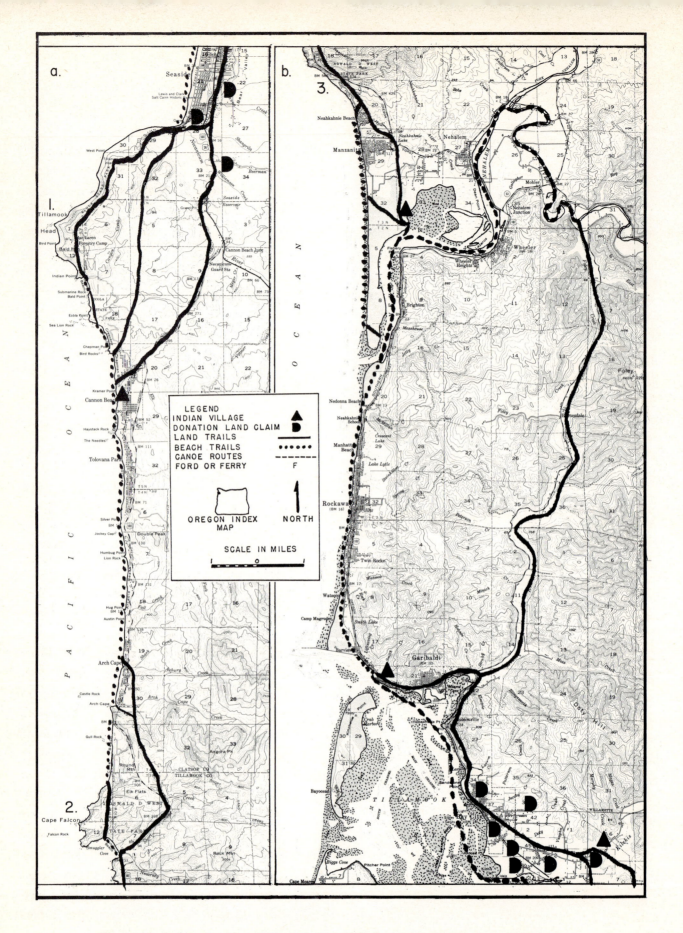

Fig. 11. Trails from Seaside to Tillamook. The chief obstacles in this area were Tillamook Head (1), Cape Falcon (2), and Neahkahnie Mountain (3). Base map: Cannon Beach (a) and Nehalem (b) quadrangles. Coast Survey charts T 1382 (1868) and T 1416 (1875), and Land Office maps T5N R10W (1856), T4N R10W (1893), and T3N R10W (1858).

Fig. 12. Photo of Tillamook Head (left) and Ecola Park area. William Clark found trails in this area slippery in wet weather. (Oregon State Highway photo) *Fig. 13* at right above is portion of old Topographic Chart T 1382b (1874), showing trails near present Seaside. Here the southbound traveler, if afoot, could turn west and take the short trail across Tillamook Head, or continue up the Necanicum River, cross to Circle Creek, and eventually reach Cannon Beach. Where terrain permitted there was usually more than one version of the Coast Trail.

ing and then, crossing the swamps and dunes to the beach, traveled south on the beach to Necanicum River (Fig. 13), which he called Clatsop River. This he crossed and visited the salt-making operation on the beach near the foot of "Tillamook Mountain," as he described it. From there, with an Indian guide, Clark's small party traveled westward along the beach over the cobbles and boulders. This is difficult walking, particularly if people are carrying packs. Clark says he traveled in this direction for two and one-half miles which probably is an exaggeration, since this would bring him to a point where at present, at least, it is not feasible to travel even at low tide. They ascended the steep cliff, probably about one and one-half miles west of Seaside. This trail (Fig. 14) slanted steeply up the cliff and brought them to the eminence known as Tillamook Head, the highest point. Here Clark had a splendid view, including Cape Disappointment on the north side of the Columbia River. Then they continued along the edge of the cliffs, along a line later developed as part of the Ecola Park Trail, to the westernmost point of the headland where another good view was obtained. After continuing for a short distance, they camped near a small creek. The next day they continued their travel down the south side of Tillamook Head and arrived at Indian Beach. From this point Clark describes the travel over three "dismal points," now called Ball Point, Ecola Point, and Chapman Point. Clark noted the landslides in this area which make it especially difficult to travel. It had

Fig. 14. A portion of the old chart of the northern part of Tillamook Head, showing trails (dash lines) south of Seaside. (U.S. Coast Survey Chart 788, OHS, by J. J. Gilbert, 1874)

rained heavily the day before, so that the trail was slippery.

South of Chapman Point he traveled "two miles along the beach" to Elk Creek which he called Ecola Creek; actually this distance is about one mile. The party crossed Elk Creek and reached the stranded whale which was the principal object of the trip. Clark measured the whale by pacing and found it to be 105 feet long, perhaps something of an exaggeration. The party returned by the same route in one day with 300 pounds of blubber purchased from the Tillamook Indians.

Two additional trails crossed Tillamook Head, one in the middle and one on the east (see Fig. 14). The east trail was undoubtedly the easiest from the standpoint of terrain, but it was the longest and apparently the traveler had greater difficulties with vegetation. It led from the south end of the beach at Seaside, southeasterly, then followed Circle Creek, undoubtedly at times following the creek bed. This trail was followed in part by J. H. Frost in August, 1841, when he crossed the area on his way from Clatsop Plains to the Willamette Valley. In Frost's day difficulties were encountered with dense vegetation; "the briers, and bushes were ten or twelve feet high, and very thickly interwoven."[18] Frost chose the east trail on the advice of the Indians who said that the pack horse could not manage the west trail. Apparently Frost left Circle Creek a few miles south of Seaside, climbed a ridge and joined the middle trail. There is little recorded evidence that the middle trail was used in the early days, but it was shown quite distinctly on the U.S. Coast Survey Chart (T 1382b) of 1874. This middle trail was the most direct route from Seaside to Cannon Beach and did not climb to high elevations as did the western trail.

All three trails brought the traveler to the beach, the west trail reaching Indian Beach, from which a trail about one mile long crossed Indian Point, Ecola Point, and Chapman Point to Elk Creek.

From Elk Creek southward (Fig. 15) the beach was easy going except at Humbug Point, Hug Point (Fig. 16), and Arch Cape. This part of the beach was used as a highway in the days of the stagecoaches and some improvements were made by blasting the rock at Hug Point, so that it could be passed at mid-tide. In the south part of the area there were two trails over Cape Falcon (Fig. 17); one, the short trail, about a mile long, took the traveler down the beach as far as possible, then crossed to the north end of Short Sand Beach. The other trail, leaving the beach to the north of Arch Cape, followed along the crest of the ridges until it reached Short Sand Creek.

Neahkahnie Mountain (Fig. 18) was the terror of travelers, particularly those with pack animals. It is a rugged headland, 1,700 feet high, protruding into the ocean, composed of basalt, sandstone, and shale. The western slope of the mountain from its crest is as steep as the roof of a house and as it approaches the sea the slope breaks off in an almost vertical cliff, nearly 500 feet above the sea. The slope of the mountain would be comparatively easy to negotiate if it were not so stony. Actually, most of the surface is made up of old rock slides which have been covered with thin vegetation, mostly grasses and salal. Frost describes the mountain as a prairie, which it was in his time. Now it is covered in part with brush and trees. But throughout the grass, brush and tree areas, the present-day hiker on the slopes of Neahkahnie finds very poor footing.

The Indian trail followed by the early settlers left the beach at Short Sand and, climbing gradually, followed a trough-like depression for some distance. As it approached the steepest area, the trail hovered at the very edge of the cliff in order that the traveler should not climb any higher than necessary. The Indians followed this path but it was not suitable for livestock. Frost described it as being about the "width of a man's

Fig. 16 (left). Postcard view shows the road blasted through Hug Point south of Cannon Beach. Earlier the point was passed by foot travelers at low tide. Below is 1968 photo from west, with remnants of road still visible (Ore. State Highway photo).

Fig. 17, right top, is view north from Neahkahnie Mountain, showing the location of the trail. Cape Falcon in the distance, beyond Treasure Cove. (OHS photo collection) *Fig. 18,* right, below, shows northern approach to Neahkahnie Mountain. It was comparatively easy (left of view). The difficult portion (right, dashed line) was obliterated by road construction. (Ore. State Highway photo)

NO 506 CAPE FALCON & TREASURE COVE ON TRAIL NEAH-KAH-NIE MT. NEAR NEHALEM ORE.

Fig. 15. Cannon Beach and Tillamook Head from south. Once the traveler from the Clatsop Plains had crossed Tillamook Head, the beach provided an easy route south to Cape Falcon, with only minor detours at Hug Point, and Arch Cape (Ore. State Highway photo).

Fig. 20. The first road over Neahkahnie Mountain (Gifford Col., OHS).

two hands, stony and gravelly." By ascending the mountain a little higher and farther from the ocean, a somewhat easier passage was found, but even here the stony nature of the ground made for poor footing, even though the surface was grassed over.

Later a relatively safe trail (Figs. 19 and 20) was established, and still later a modern road (Fig. 21). But for many years Neahkahnie Mountain was the most dreaded point on the Oregon Coast. The story is told of a trip across Neahkahnie Mountain after the mail route was established. The mail carrier agreed to escort a horseman across the mountain, but the latter, seeing the steep slope, became so frightened that it was necessary for the mailman to tie his feet underneath the horse and blindfold him before the passage could be effected. Frost's passage across the mountain required the better part of two days and he filled five (printed) pages of his journal in describing the journey. In view of the difficulties of the Neahkahnie Mountain trail it is likely that alternate routes were used and there is some physical evidence that a trail led around the east side of Neahkahnie Mountain, but no record has been found of travelers using this trail.

On the south side of Neahkahnie Mountain, the trail divided (see Fig. 22), and one part reached the beach north of the present town of Manzanita where the sandy area begins.[19] To the north of this the beach contains cobbles and boulders derived from the erosion

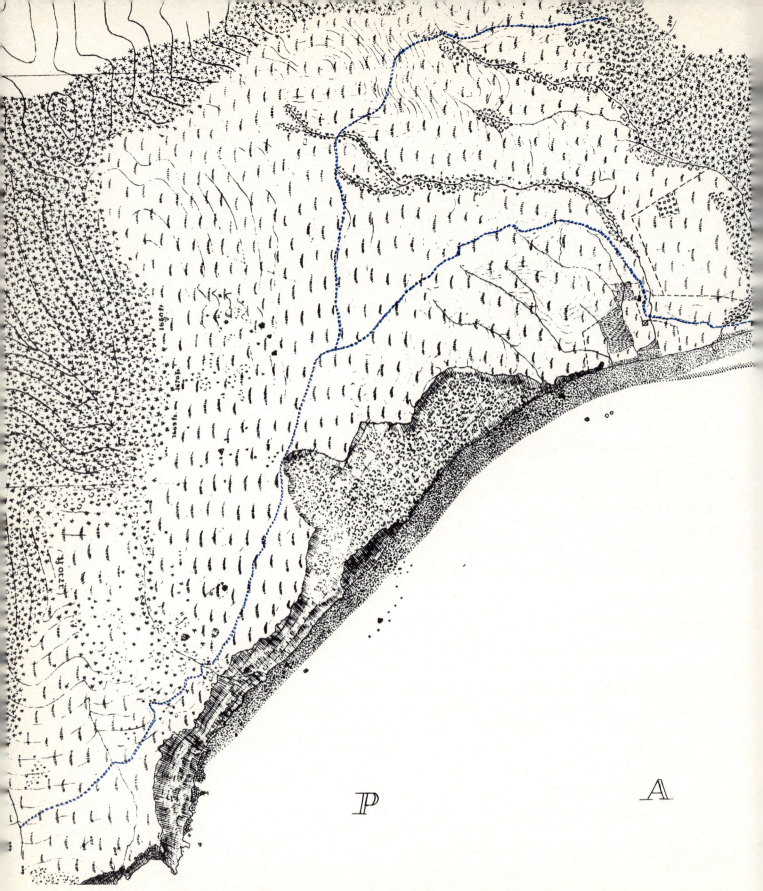

Fig. 22. Old chart showing trail on the south side of Neahkahnie Mountain (in blue). (U.S. Coast Survey Chart T 1461b (782, OHS), 1875)

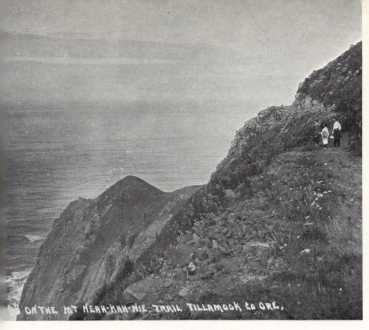 

Fig. 19, left, shows improved trail over Neahkahnie Mountain (OHS). *Fig. 21* (right): The construction of a modern road over Neahkahnie Mountain completely obliterated most of the old trail. (Ore. State Highway photo)

of Neahkahnie cliffs, and is not suitable for travel. The beach trail led all the way down the sandspit to a point near the outlet of Nehalem Bay where a ferry was necessary to reach the south shore. The other trail continued inland to the east of Manzanita and reached the bay about two miles above the outlet near an Indian village, opposite Fishery Point (see Fig. 8). Perhaps it was the presence of the Indian village that led the trail to this point, since here a canoe ferry could be obtained. This was a convenience to early travelers, who were usually taken across Nehalem Bay in Indian canoes, swimming their horses behind them. (But Warren Vaughn waited three days in the empty, flea-infested village for a canoe; all the Indians were up-river picking berries.) The water route took the traveler to the outlet of the bay, since the eastern shore of the lower bay does not have a good beach for travel and the adjacent upland is rugged.

South of Nehalem Bay the traveler had the choice of two relatively easy, parallel routes, one along the beach to Tillamook Bay, another a short distance inland, following closely the route of Highway 101. The inner route was preferred at high tide but was often quite muddy in winter. An alternate trail led up the Nehalem River several miles above the bay, up Foley Creek, and down the Miami River to Tillamook Bay (see Fig. 23); this was on the mail route from Astoria to Tillamook. Boats were used from the lower bay, up the Nehalem River, to the mouth of Foley Creek and thence the journey was by land, since neither Foley Creek nor the upper reaches of Miami River were navigable. Although the trails in the Nehalem area were used by many travelers after 1850, no permanent settlement was made here until the 1860s.[20]

The Tillamook Area

The Tillamook Area (Fig. 23) extends from Barview and Garibaldi on the north to Cape Lookout on the south. This area was very attractive to early settlers for a number of reasons, mainly because of the plain, the bay, and the rivers. Perhaps the most striking feature was the alluvial plain, so unusual in the coastal area. This plain of irregular shape extends from Bay City on the north to South Prairie on the south, a distance of eight miles. The plain is about six miles wide. Most of the plain ranges in elevation from 20 to 50 feet. Tillamook Bay, trending to the northwest, is about two and one-half to three miles wide

[25]

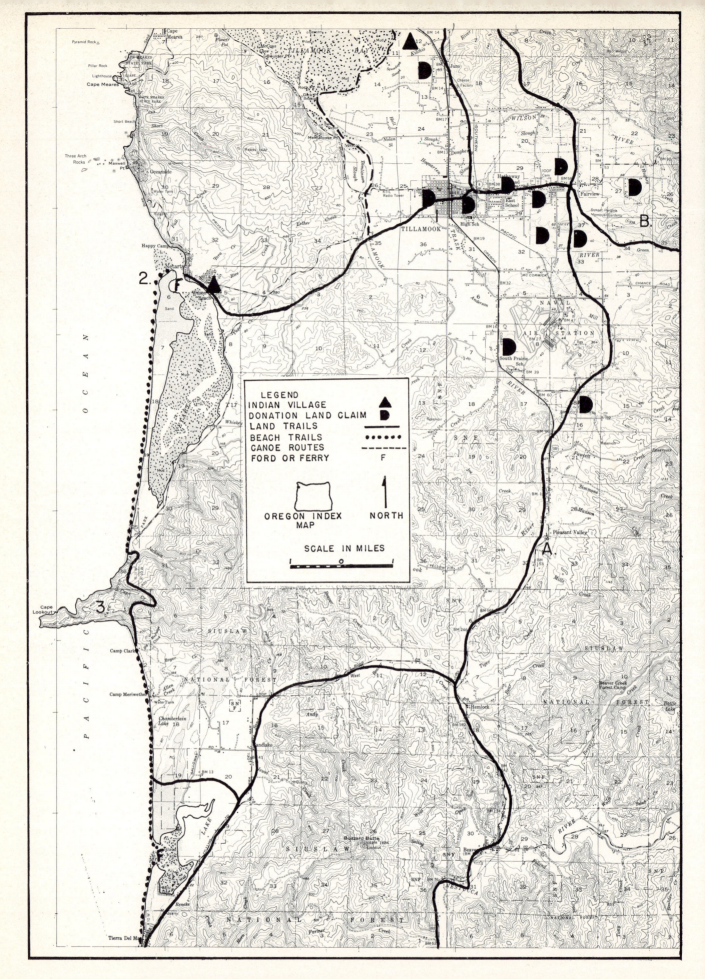

Fig. 23. Trails in the Tillamook area. Early travelers turned west from Tillamook (1) to Netarts Bay (2), and followed the beach to Cape Lookout (3). Later an inland trail (A) was cleared providing a more direct route to the Willamette Valley. Still later another trail (B) was laid out due east from Tillamook. Base map: Tillamook Quadrangle. Land Office maps T1S R10W (1858) and T2S R10W (1858).

Fig. 24. Airphoto of a part of the western margin of the Tillamook Plain (just west of town), showing the Tillamook River and tributary channels. Netarts Landing (N) was a crossing place from which a trail led west to Netarts on the coast. (U.S. Corps of Engineers photo, 1939)

and about five miles long. It has a number of coves or intermediate bays, giving the shoreline an irregular outline. Channels in the bay made it easy for the small boats and ships of the early days to navigate, but the tidal flats in a number of places, particularly in the south end of the bay, restricted the landings and made travel along the shore difficult. Fishing was important; for many years after settlement the people depended on salmon and potatoes for their principal subsistence.

The Tillamook Plain is the focus of a number of rivers. Beginning on the north with the Garibaldi area, the Miami River enters the bay. It has a narrow floodplain which as used as an alternate route of travel to the north, as noted above. Other rivers entering the bay include the Kilchis, Wilson, Trask, and Tillamook,

Rugged Cape Meares was bypassed by early travelers. A land trail and a canoe route led along the east side of Tillamook Bay (upper part of photo). (Ore. State Highway photo)

and each of these in their lower courses has a floodplain which afforded sites for early settlers. The lower courses of all these rivers are tidal and they are bordered by tidal flats (Fig. 24). These tidal flats presented some difficulty to travel in the early days, particularly if pack horses or other livestock were involved. Livestock tended to get mired.[21]

One of the features of the Tillamook area that appealed to the early settlers was the prairies, some in the plain, some at higher elevations. These prairies were covered either with grass or bracken fern, easy to clear and put under cultivation, which was an important factor. On the surrounding hills, especially near the ocean, Sitka spruce was the common tree; a bit inland Douglas fir and cedar were common. All of these trees were used by the early settlers in building their houses, boats, and ships.

To the west of Tillamook Bay is Bayocean Peninsula, almost closing the channel entrance, which is about one-fourth of a mile wide. This peninsula is hummocky in the south, low and flat in the north. After the construction of the jetty in 1918 the sea began to erode the peninsula and eventually broke through the southern section into the bay. This break

Fig. 25. Like Cape Meares, Maxwell Point just to the south, had no trails in the early days. Cape Lookout in the distance. (Ore. State Highway photo)

was mended by a long dike. To the south of Bayocean Peninsula is the rugged headland of Cape Meares and to the south of this is Maxwell Point (Fig. 25). There is no indication that a trail was used for travel to any great extent in the early days, and only within the last few years has a roadway been constructed from Cape Meares southward to Oceanside.

To the south of Cape Meares is Netarts Bay and Netarts Peninsula, the spit which separates the bay from the ocean. The entrance to Netarts Bay is narrow also, and this enabled the early travelers to ferry across in canoes and continue down the beach. On the south-western part of the area is Cape Lookout (Figs. 26, 27), a long, narrow finger of cape, with a very steep slope on the south and a fairly rugged slope on the north.

Surrounding the Tillamook Plain on all sides except the bay side are low hills, most of which are based on sandstone and shale. In general, these are not rugged nor are they very high in elevation. The greatest difficulty, from the standpoint of travel, was the dense vegetation that covered most of the area in the early days.

The Tillamook Indians were living at various points around the bay and at other localities when the

Fig. 26. Cape Lookout was crossed by a fairly easy trail as shown (approximately) by the white line. (See Fig. 13.) (Ore. State Highway photo)

first white settlers arrived. There was a village at the entrance of the bay on the north side in the vicinity of Barview, one at Kilchis Point on the east side of the bay, and another on the Kilchis River, about two miles to the east. The Indians were of great help to the white settlers in a number of ways. Their trails became the trails of the white man; they acted as guides, and they actually transported people at various points, particularly over water. They helped with the cattle drives and supplied fish to the early settlers. Undoubtedly the early history of Tillamook would have been very different if the Indians had been hostile or if there had been no Indians at all.

The first settler, Joseph C. Champion, came by sea in 1851. Most of the others for the next few years came by land. They settled at various points on the plain, but mostly in the western area. Warren Vaughn took a donation land claim at the present site of Ida-

Fig. 27. South of Cape Lookout the trail followed the beach for a short distance and then detoured inland around Sand Lake (see Fig. 28). (Ore. State Highway photo)

ville, to the southeast of Bay City. In a few years there were eight donation land claims located in the prairie areas but near the west side of the plain. This suggests that the settlers were very much oriented to fishing as well as to agriculture. In 1854 Warren Vaughn took a census of the settlers and found that there were 80 people living in the plain.[22] The U.S. census of 1860 counted 95 for Tillamook County.

Most of the settlers who came to the Tillamook area by land used one of two routes. In the north they came in from Astoria having reached that point by boat from Oregon City and Fort Vancouver. From the south they came across the Coast Range from the Willamette Valley and the upper Yamhill drainage, specifically the tributary Rogue River, and reached the drainage of the Nestucca River to the south of Tillamook Bay, thence north along the coast to Netarts and across the hills to Tillamook Bay. These routes

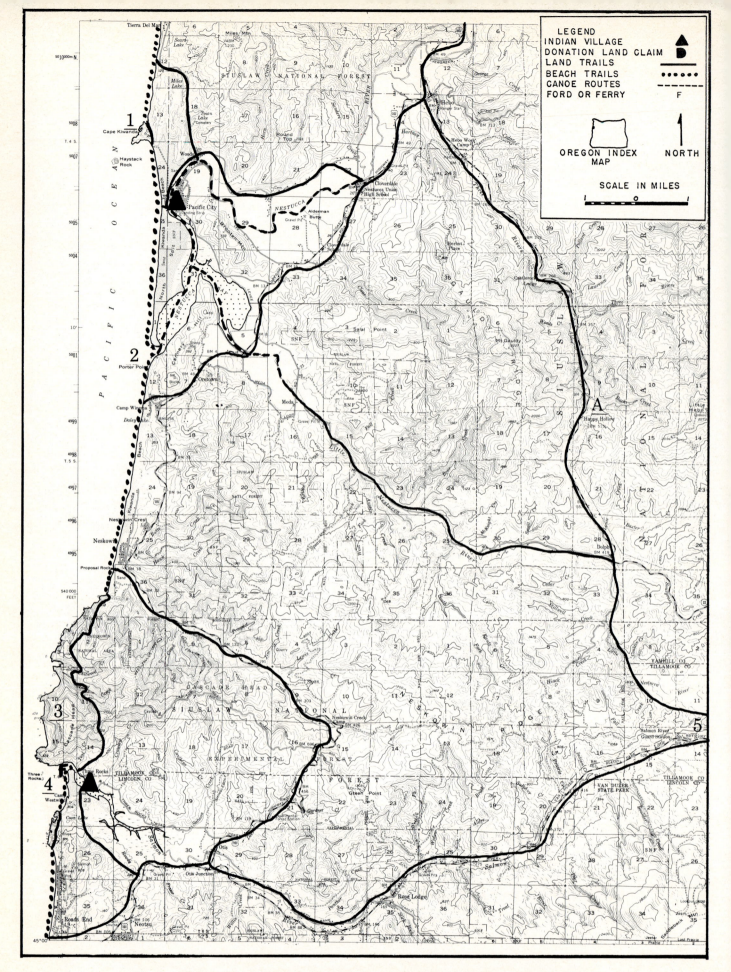

Fig. 28. Trails of the Nestucca area. Earliest travel was along the shore, crossing Cape Kiwanda (1), the Nestucca River (2), and Cascade Head (3) to the Salmon River (4). From this point most travelers turned eastward to the Willamette Valley. After 1853 most travelers used the inland route (A) which joined the Salmon River route near Grand Ronde (5). Base map: Hebo Quadrangle. Land Office map T6S R10W (1890).

were known to the Indians, were pointed out by Indian guides, and for the first few years were the only land routes used. The entire route, both north and south, was followed by J. H. Frost,[23] who traveled from Clatsop Plains down through Tillamook, over the Nestucca area to the Willamette Valley. When he and his companions, Solomon H. Smith and Lewis Taylor, an Indian guide, and a pack horse, reached Tillamook Bay (which Frost called a river) near Barview, some of the horse's pack was transferred to two Indian canoes and Frost, Taylor, and the baggage were ferried to the south end of Tillamook Bay. Frost's companion, Smith, with an Indian guide, took the horse around by land, however, and made almost as good time as did the canoe, moving against the tide.

Smith's route, along the east shore of the bay, passed the present sites of Garibaldi and Bay City. It was not difficult; in many places the beach could be followed, but in other places the beach was not passable at high tide and so the travelers had to climb up over the headlands or go through the brush and trees adjacent to the bay. It was necessary to travel around Miami Cove, cross four rivers, and the tidal marshes. From time to time Frost landed and assisted in getting the horse and pack over the rivers. From the Kilchis River, Smith traveled generally south, passed near the site of the present city of Tillamook, and reached the southwest side of the plain on the lower Tillamook River at a point later known to the pioneers as Netarts Landing, because the trail led westward from here to Netarts Bay.

Frost was confused by the numerous rivers to be crossed and states that "we crossed the river four times and then crossed it again." In foggy weather, of course, one could easily mistake one river for another or five rivers for one. The Indian guide suggested that the easiest time to cross the rivers was at high tide because at this time less of the tidal marsh was exposed. This presumably meant that the horse was swimming across the deepest part of the river. Having crossed at Netarts Landing, Frost and party continued westward to Netarts. This well-traveled trail led along a ridge to the south of the present paved road that crosses Cape Meares Peninsula. Arrived at Netarts and awaiting a low tide, the party was ferried over to the sandspit in an Indian canoe. Frost referred to the outlet of Netarts Bay as a river, just as he had referred to Tillamook Bay as a river, when he first observed it at the outlet. From the spit the party traveled southward along the beach to the foot of Cape Lookout. Cape Lookout was crossed by a winding trail, looping eastward around the valley of Cape Creek and descending to the beach on the south side (see Figs. 23 and 27). From this point the beach trail led south to the Sand Lake area.

The trail used by Frost in this area was, with some small variations, the usual trail for several years after the first settlers arrived. Most of them came up the Yamhill, across the Coast Range, and down the Salmon River, thence north to Tillamook. This route was long and roundabout and, because of brush and vegetation, difficult to follow. Both Frost and Vaughn were lost on this trail more than once even though they had traveled the trail previously with an Indian guide. Even Indian guides sometimes got lost if they traveled more than a day's journey from their home village. Soon an effort was made to shorten this trail. In 1854, according to Warren Vaughn's Journal,[24] a trail was cleared leading south from the Tillamook Plain, more specifically from Hoquarten Prairie, on the east side of the plain, using the valley of the Tillamook River, passing through the settlement known as Pleasant Valley and then following Beaver Creek to the Nestucca River to the area of the present Hebo. From Hebo the trail was cleared up Three Rivers to the present Dolph, thence to the town of Grand Ronde, and headquarters of the Indian reservation. Clearing the trail from the north end was the work of the peo-

Fig. 30. Cascade Head and the Salmon River. A trail from the Willamette Valley joined the Coast Trail here. (Univ. of California Engineers photo)

ple of Tillamook, while Willamette Valley settlers cleared the south end. It is one of the first accounts of the actual clearing of a trail of this magnitude. Vaughn relates that after clearing the brush and making the route passable for people and livestock, there still remained 200 deadfalls across the trail which could not be removed because of the lack of saws.

The easiest way to get to Tillamook was undoubtedly by water, from Oregon City or Portland, down the Columbia River to Astoria, and then by land or sea. But the opportunity for travel by sea occurred at irregular intervals. Ships were scarce, the bar was dangerous, and several wrecks were recorded. For many years most of the people and livestock moved in and out of Tillamook on the trails.

The Nestucca Area

South of Lookout Point the trail followed the beach to the Nestucca River (Fig. 28), bypassing Sand Lake, where Warren Vaughn got his cattle mired in the quicksand.[25] Nearly all the trails were related to travel between Tillamook and the Willamette Valley and as the early travelers crossed this area they found only Indian villages, mainly at Pacific City and at the outlet of the Salmon River.

Fig. 29. An Indian village, near the present site of Pacific City (center), provided canoes to cross the Nestucca River. Later an inland trail was established, leading to Tillamook (white line, upper right), and another northward from the settlement of Woods (W) to bypass Cape Kiwanda. (Univ. of California Engineers photo)

Beginning at the north at Tierra del Mar, the south-bound traveler found a good beach as far as Cape Kiwanda, which was easy to bypass on the dunes. This brought the traveler again to the beach, which could be traveled to a point where the Nestucca River approaches the beach (now Pacific City) (Fig. 29). The Indians living on the east side of the river provided canoes so that the traveler could be ferried across the river, but, if he were continuing southward, he could disembark near the outlet of Nestucca Bay near the present Porter Point. Thence the traveler had a fine beach southward for several miles to Cascade Head.

The journey over Cascade Head (Fig. 30) was difficult, not only because of the steepness of the trail but because of brush and mud. But cattle were driven over this trail by Frost in 1841 and a number of other travelers, including Warren Vaughn, passed this particular point. It was possible to ford the Salmon River at low tide, but canoes were available at an Indian village on the north shore to ferry passengers and goods. Livestock, including pack animals, could swim or wade depending upon the tide. South of the Salmon River a short beach led to a small promontory (Fig. 31) which could be passed over easily since the upper part of it was flat and in the nature of a terrace. From this point the sand beach led southward for about 15 miles to the Siletz River.

[35]

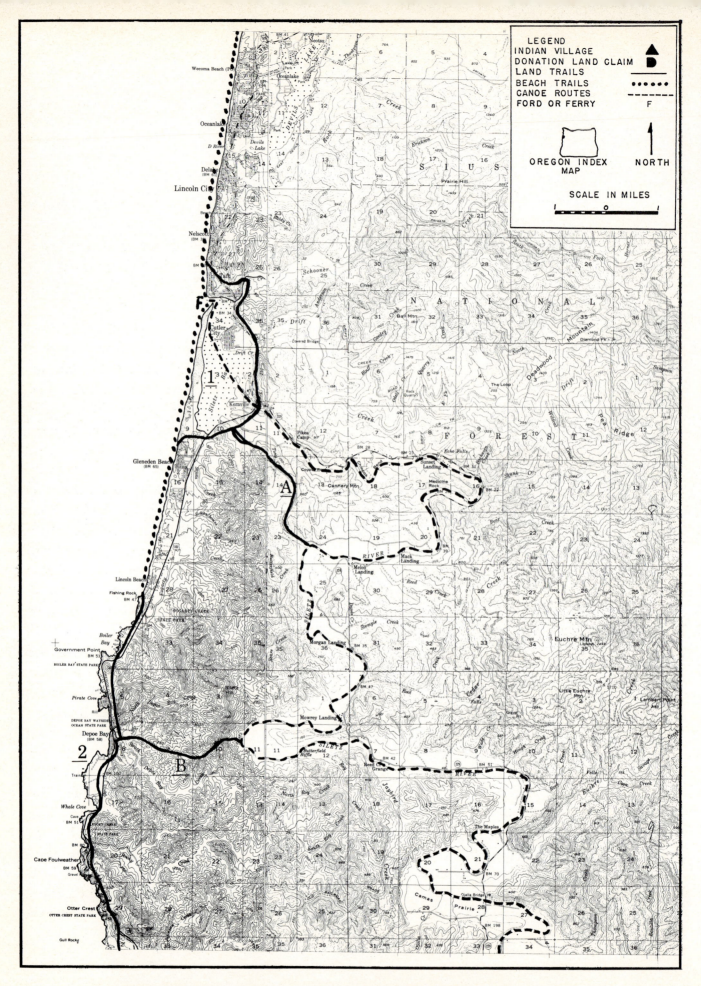

Fig. 32. Trails of the Siletz area. Travel was near the shore or inland along the Siletz River. Short trails (A) and (B) connected the river with Siletz Bay (1) and Depoe Bay (2). Base map: Cape Foulweather and Euchre Mountain quadrangles. Coast Survey Chart T 1086 (1868) and Land Office maps T9S R10W (1875) and T9S R11W (1875).

Trails of the Middle Oregon Coast

As noted above, the middle portion of the Oregon Coast, from the Siletz River to the Siuslaw River, was settled at a later date than either the north or south portions and, as a consequence, fewer trails were used. Most of the travel was by exploring parties or in connection with the Indian reservation which occupied a large portion of the area. It is also clear that this section was not particularly attractive to early settlers;[26] good agricultural land was very scarce and even today most of the settlement is related to logging or recreation. Another reason for the scarcity of trails was the easy beach travel. Only a few small headlands and river crossings interrupted the long, nearly straight beaches (Figs. 32, 33, 34 and 35).

The Siletz-Yaquina Area

The northern portion of the middle Oregon Coast extends from Devils Lake to Seal Rocks and includes portions of the Cape Foulweather, Euchre Mountain, Yaquina, and Toledo quadrangles. Two-thirds of the Siletz area, from Devils Lake down to Otter Crest, provided easy beach travel with one ferry or ford necessary at the outlet of Siletz Bay. In most of this area it was also easy to travel slightly above the beach on a low terrace, in case the tide was high; the accounts of the early travelers indicate that this was often done.[27]

The Siletz and Yaquina rivers provided alternate routes. As previously indicated, travelers preferred to travel along a small river parallel to the coast rather than along the beach, and if the river was navigable by canoe or small boat, so much the better. This was the case of the Siletz River, particularly north of the reservation agency at the town of Siletz. Also, the upper Siletz River provided a land route eastward to the Willamette Valley, not one of the best nor easiest routes across the Coast Range, but one of the most direct from the standpoint of the reservation. The Siletz River, as the map shows (see Fig. 32), meanders in a very irregular manner across the area and, although it did not supply a direct route, it was obviously used, as indicated by place names such as Mowrey Landing, Morgan Landing, Mack Landing, and Sunset Landing. Probably this river valley was used as a land route as well. Another factor suggesting the reason for using this interior route was that the earliest settlers found small areas of good farming land on the prairies and tributary valleys and naturally the traveler tended to gravitate to these settlements, rather than to travel along the coast where settlements were few. The lower Siletz River was connected to the coast by at least two trails (see Fig. 32), one to Depoe Bay and another to the south side of Siletz Bay.

Southward from the Siletz River (Fig. 36), a short land route led to Depoe ("Depot") Slough (not to be confused with Depoe Bay), a tributary of the Yaquina

Fig. 35 (above). The first road across Cape Foulweather followed the old trail, portions of which can be seen in this photo (OHS Collections). *Fig. 31* (below). The coast south of the Salmon River forced the traveler to cross over the hills. Short beaches, such as this one (Crescent Beach), were not very useful, especially at high tide. (Oregon State Highway photo)

Fig. 34, above, shows the coast at Otter Rock. Too rugged for a trail, the beach to the south was used. Yaquina Head in the middle distance (Ore. State Highway photo). *Fig. 33* (below). The coast near Whale Cove, Lincoln County, is not very rugged but nevertheless the trail was located inland on the terrace. A few short beaches were of little use to the traveler. (Gifford Col., OHS)

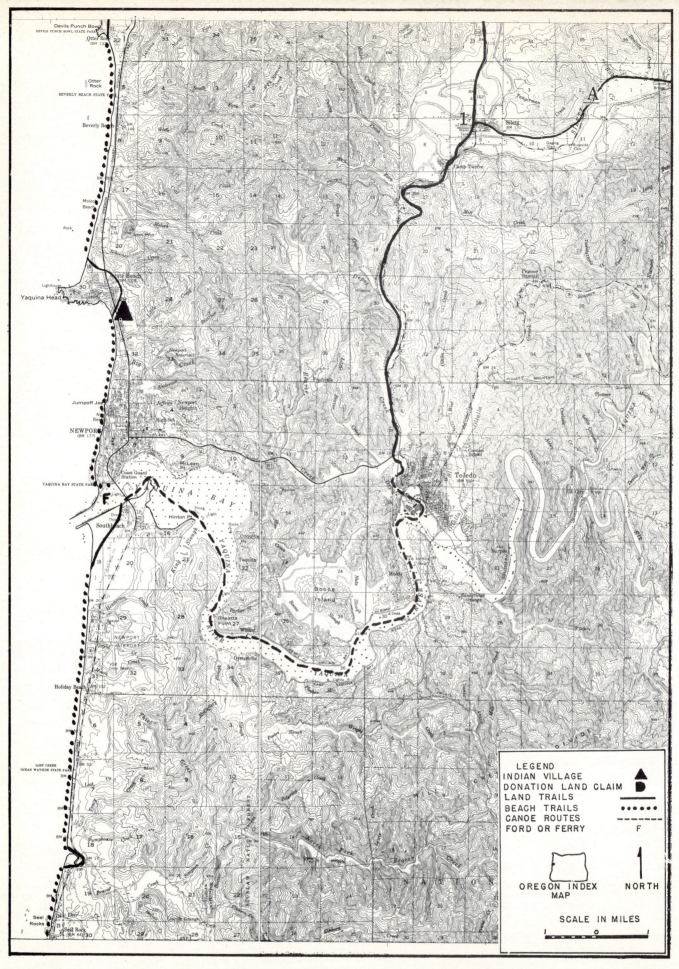

Fig. 36. Trails of the Yaquina area. The inland trail served the Siletz Indian Reservation (1). The trail to the east (A), leading to the Willamette Valley, was cleared by the U.S. Army. Base map: Yaquina and Toledo quadrangles. Coast Survey Chart 775 OHS (1868) and Land Office maps T9S R11W (1875) and T10S R10W (1877).

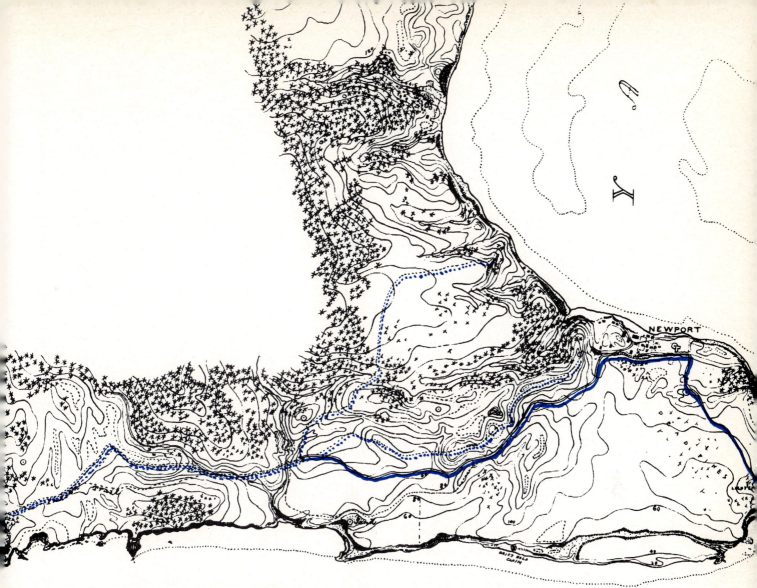

Fig. 37. A portion of the old chart of Yaquina Bay showing the trail to the north and south (in blue). Yaquina Head (front cover) is at left edge. (U.S. Coast Survey Chart T 1086 (OHS 775), 1868)

River. The lower part of this slough is tidewater and, when Corporal Royal Bensell made this trip in the 1860s,[28] a barge was used to transport horses while a small boat was used to carry the troops who were headed down the coast in search of deserting Indians. After landing on the south side of Yaquina Bay near the ocean, the troops rode southward on the terrace near the beach.

The traveler who elected to follow the coast, rather than the Siletz-Yaquina route, had to leave the beach at Fishing Rock, north of Boiler Bay, and travel on the terraces and over the comparatively low headland of Cape Foulweather. The trail followed close upon the old route of Highway 101, which is at a lower elevation than the present highway. Having passed Otter Rock (Yaquina Quadrangle), the traveler again encountered several miles of good beach; then it was necessary to pass Yaquina Head. This was done by a short trail near an Indian village. Undoubtedly the Indians had marked out a clear trail in this area. Thence the trail continued down the beach to Yaquina Bay (Fig. 37) (Newport), where it was necessary to ferry across the Yaquina River, although at low tide it could be forded. South of Yaquina Bay, the traveler could follow the beach or the terrace to Alsea Bay with only one short detour around Seal Rocks.

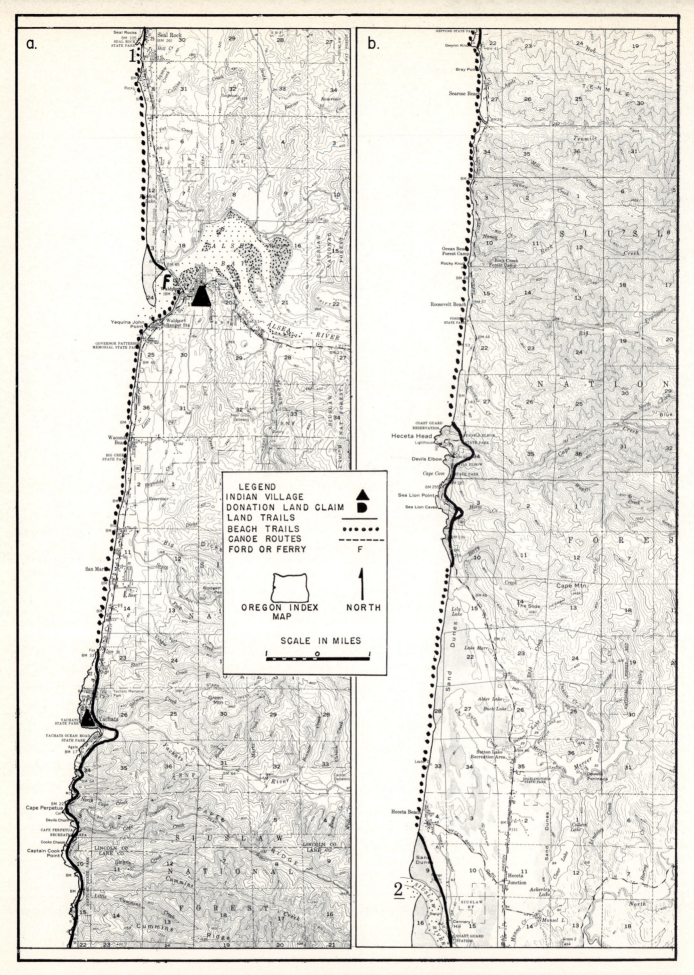

Fig. 38. Trail from Seal Rocks (1) to the Siuslaw River (2). The trail left the beach only to pass over headlands or to find easier crossings of the rivers. Base map: Waldport (a) and Heceta Head (b) quadrangles. Coast Survey charts T 1810 (1887) and T 1811 (1887), and Land Office maps T14S R11W (1883), T14S R12W (1879), and T16S R12W (1883).

Fig. 40. Storms like this one at Neptune State Park, four miles south of Yachats, made the rocky shore unsafe to travel. (Gifford Col., OHS)

The Alsea-Heceta Head Area

The coast from Seal Rocks on the north to the Siuslaw River on the south (Fig. 38) presents a smooth, even beach except for a few headlands, Cape Perpetua, Heceta Head, and Sea Lion Point. This coast was traveled by A. R. McLeod,[29] a representative of the Hudson's Bay Company, in 1826 and described in some detail. It was also traversed by Corporal Bensell in his journey from the Siletz Indian Reservation southward to Coos Bay.

A short detour across the North Spit of Alsea Bay brought the travelers to a point near the present highway bridge. Some of the early travelers forded the bay at low tide, but Indian canoes were available to carry people across. From this point a continuous beach stretched southward almost to Yachats. At Yachats in the early days there was an Indian agency, and Bensell reported about 600 Indians living there. The coast at Yachats for about one mile both north and south is very rocky, so that it was necessary to travel along the terrace. The route crossed the Yachats River near the present highway bridge and then followed along the terrace which leads southward for about one mile to the slopes of Cape Perpetua.

Cape Perpetua offered no very serious handicap to foot travelers. By keeping very near the shore, particularly at low tide, it was possible to pass the cape

Fig. 39. This much-photographed view from Cape Perpetua (named by Captain Cook, 1778) illustrates the trail choices of early travelers. The low route, preferred by Indians, led along the rocky bench and called for a little wading. The upper route (white line) avoided the deepest parts of the little canyons, such as Cook's Chasm. (Ore. State Highway photo)

Fig. 42. Sea Lion Point was difficult to cross because of the steep cliff on the north, extending eastward along Cape Creek. Remnants of the old trail can be seen along the upper part of this view. (Ore. State Highway photo)

Fig. 41. The coast near Heceta Head was difficult to follow. There the trail led inland to avoid the steep slopes. (OHS Col.)

without climbing very high. However, Bensell found this necessitated traveling over rocky shelves (Fig. 39) and negotiating several steep cliffs and it was not easy for pack animals or horseback riders.[30]

Another trail at a higher elevation was also in use. This was somewhat above the present highway in places, on the western flank of Cape Perpetua. South of Captain Cook Point the coastline is irregular (Fig. 40) and several rocky points were detoured, after which an uninterrupted series of beaches extends south to Heceta Head.

Heceta Head (Fig. 41) was not easy to pass and Sea Lion Point to the south of it was even more difficult. Particularly difficult was the climb from the bed of Cape Creek at Devil's Elbow, up the headland to the south and over Sea Lion Point (Fig. 42). Once the traveler had passed Sea Lion Point and descended to the beach, however, he could look forward to some 60 miles of continuous beach, interrupted only by streams.

Approaching the Siuslaw River, the trail left Heceta Beach and climbed up onto the wooded dunes, then continued past the present Coast Guard Station, where it was possible to use the river beach except at high tide. At this time, 1840-1862, there were no jetties at the Siuslaw River entrance and the shoreline was quite different from the present one.

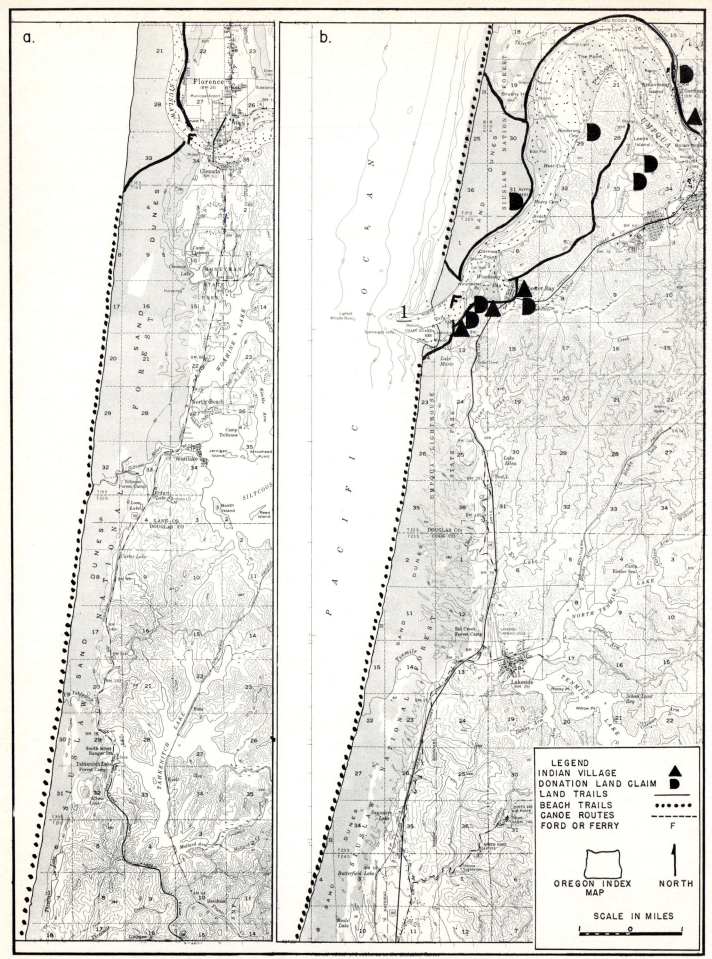

Fig. 43. Trails of the Umpqua area. The Umpqua River (1) brought many travelers to the coast from the southern end of the Willamette Valley, usually by trail to Scottsburg, thence by river craft to the coast. Base map: Siltcoos Lake (a) and Reedsport (b) quadrangles. Coast Survey Chart T 1768 (1885).

Trails of the Southern Oregon Coast

SETTLERS began to arrive in considerable numbers on the southern Oregon Coast in the early 1850s, either via the Umpqua Valley, overland from California, or by ship from Crescent City, California (founded 1853). As mentioned, many of the newcomers were seeking gold in the beach sands, in the streams, and in the terrace gravels. Doubtless every sizable beach with black sand was prospected for gold. Placer operations on the beaches were very short-lived in most places, but played an important role in attracting settlers and in the location of settlements and trails. At one time or another placers were worked at Whalehead, Pistol River, Gold Beach, Euchre Creek, Port Orford, Cape Blanco, and Randolph; also on the terrace gravels along the foothills.[31] About the same time agricultural settlements were established on the Chetco River (Brookings), on the Rogue River (Gold Beach), on the Sixes River, around Coos Bay, on the lower Umpqua River, and at many other points along the trails. The miners pioneered many temporary trails, but the main trails were related to the farms, especially the donation land claims. For a brief period, about 1852-1856, many Indian trails were used in connection with the Indian wars.[32]

THE SIUSLAW-UMPQUA AREA

The route along the coast from the Siuslaw River to the Umpqua River (Fig. 43) was easy because of the almost continuous beach. From the Siuslaw River ferry, about one mile below the present site of Florence, the route crossed the dunes to the beach. These dunes were active at the time and undoubtedly caused some difficulty to travelers. As the beach was approached, it was necessary to cross a thin ribbon of quicksand just behind the foredune. This appears as a flat, dry riverbed composed of fine sand mixed with silt which has been washed in by water from the surrounding dunes. But the quicksand did not constitute a serious hazard because it was not deep. In this stretch of the coast, and in other places as well, there are small areas of quicksands, some on the beaches themselves. These were noted by the early travelers and it was even suggested that markers be put up to warn the travelers of these areas, though there is little record that any of these caused serious danger or even inconvenience, excepting only the quicksand at Sand Lake, previously noted. The strip of level or nearly level sand south of the Siuslaw River, immediately east of the foredune, however, did provide a means of travel when the tide was high or in stormy weather. The foredune provided some protection from the offshore winds.

As the travelers approached the Umpqua River, two trails led across the spit to the river. If it was the intention of the traveler to go up the Umpqua River, he cut across the sandspit, arriving at Brushy Hill. This is the last brush or trees occurring on the spit. From

Fig. 44. An early sketch of the Army's Fort Umpqua, seen here from Umpqua River, with dunes beyond on seaward side. (From *Frank Leslie's Illustrated Newspaper,* April 24, 1858.)

this point a trail led along the right bank, that is, the north side of the Umpqua River, around the curve to Gardiner. The only difficulty here was the marshy tidal flat on which horses sometimes had heavy going. Another trail leaving the beach farther south cut across the sandspit to what was known for a time as Fort Umpqua (1856-1862) and Umpqua City. (This is not to be confused with the Fort Umpqua many miles up the river near the present site of Elkton). The fort on the lower Umpqua River (Fig. 44) near a place now indicated as Army Hill was a U.S. Army post, designed to protect the inhabitants from the Indians, and complete the defensive encirclement of the Coast Reservation on the south,[33] whereas the one near Elkton was built and maintained earlier as a fur trade post by the Hudson's Bay Company. Fort Umpqua, at Army Hill, was occupied only a short time; as previously noted, the Indian menace in southern Oregon was of comparatively short duration. Furthermore, when the paymaster arrived at Fort Umpqua to pay the troops he found no one at all at the fort—they had all gone hunting! It was feasible to ferry across the Umpqua River (Fig. 45) at several points but the favored point was about two miles above the outlet, near Winchester Bay.

The coast from the Siuslaw River to the Umpqua River was undoubtedly the easiest of all for travel. The beach was good and there were no interruptions other than the Umpqua River itself, which was not a serious one. Most of the travelers praised this route. The favorite camping spots were at the outlet of the Siltcoos River about eight miles south of the Siuslaw River and at Ten Mile Creek about seven miles south of the Umpqua River. Some of the early travelers, finding themselves between streams on the beach and desiring fresh water for camping, crossed the dunes (Fig. 46) to one of the many fresh-water lakes near the shore.

Undoubtedly some travelers followed along the edge of the timber belt which was just inland from the dunes and from one to two miles from the coast. But in terms of ease of travel, either on the dunes or through the brush, both were more difficult than following along the beaches.

Settlements in this area were widely spaced in the early days; there was no settlement on the Siuslaw River at Florence until the 1860s and, although there was a settlement at Gardiner in 1850, there were only nine donation land claims in the Umpqua area altogether, and most of these were related to fishing rather than to agriculture. The lower Umpqua area, like the lower Siuslaw area, offered little opportunity for agriculture.

The importance of the route inland from the lower Umpqua River can scarcely be exaggerated. It was and is the easiest route in this section from the coast, across

Fig. 46 (above, left). The coastal dunes, such as these south of the Umpqua River, were not used much by travelers, but stormy weather forced foot travelers to go along the edge of the dunes above the driftwood. (Univ. of California Engineers photo). *Fig. 45* (below, right). South of the Umpqua River foot travelers and stage coaches alike followed the beaches. Here travelers are transferring from the stagecoach to a rowboat to make the river crossing. (OHS Collections)

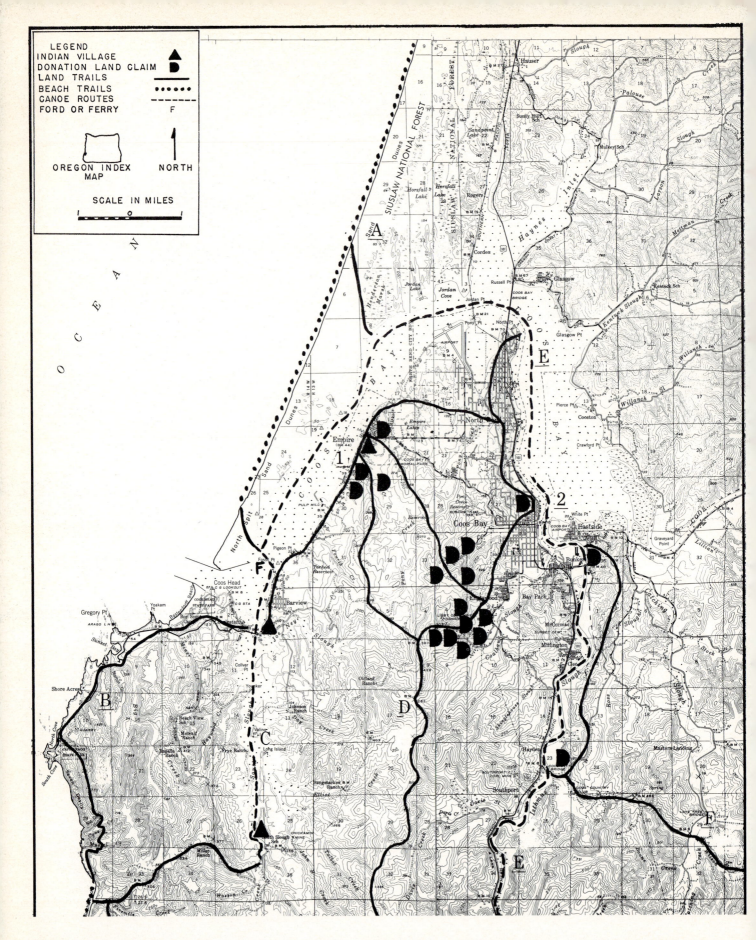

Fig. 47. Trails of the Coos Bay area. A variety of routes were used, depending on the mode of travel. Trail (A) followed the beach and brought many travelers from the Umpqua River. Trail (B) was difficult because of terrain and vegetation and was little used. Trail (C) left the beach near Five Mile Creek and ran eastward to the south end of South Slough. At this point water transportation was available. Trail (D) was the Randolph Trail connecting Empire (1) with the mining settlement to the south (see Fig. 17). Route (E) was all water except for a short portage; it connected Empire and Marshfield (2) with the Coquille River (see Fig. 17). Route (F) led to Roseburg on the Oregon-California Trail. Base Map: Empire and Coos Bay quadrangles. Coast Survey Chart T 1970 (1889) and Land Office maps T25S R13W (1857) and T26S R13W (1857).

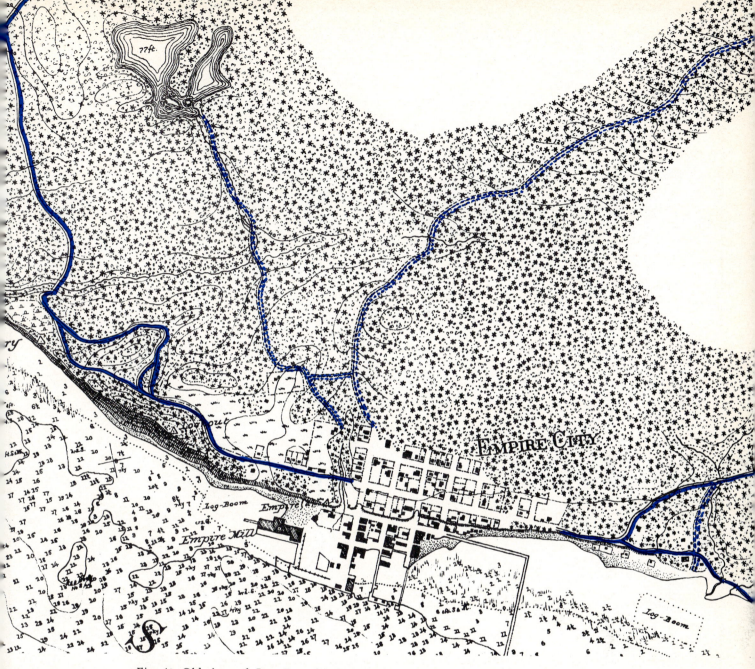

Fig. 49. Old chart of Coos Bay, showing Empire City and trail to south, in blue. (U.S. Coast Survey Chart 1971 T, 1889 (OHS 273), surveyed by E. F. Dickins and F. Westdahl.)

the Coast Range, to the Willamette Valley. The river is almost a water-level route, cutting entirely through the Coast Range. Travelers ascending the river could travel by small boats, in later years by steamers, as far as Scottsburg at the head of tide. From this point it was necessary to use small boats, such as Indian canoes, which had to be pulled through the rapids or portaged around them. The trip could be made from Scottsburg up to the fur post of Fort Umpqua, near the present site of Elkton, in one day. From Scottsburg a trail, later a roadway, led upriver via Fort Umpqua to the middle Umpqua Valley (Roseburg) where there were many donation land claims and settlements in the early days. Apparently most travelers preferred the water route, at least until the wagon road was built.

Fig. 48. The steamboat replaced the Indian canoe for river travel and the stage coaches used the beaches and improved trails. The exchange of passengers above occurred on the south shore of Coos Bay. The aerial view of Coos Bay, below, shows Cape Arago and the bay jetties. (OHS Collections)

The Coos Bay-Coquille Area

In the vicinity of Coos Bay and the lower Coquille River the pattern of trails (Figs. 47 and 50) was established in the period 1850-1860. The area stretches along the coast from the vicinity of the present town of Hauser, south to Four Mile Creek. Placer mining, coal mining, and agricultural settlements all played a role. Access to this area from the Willamette Valley was mainly via the Umpqua Valley, from Roseburg on the Oregon-California Trail; from the south and from the north access was along the coast. Shipping played an important part from the earliest times.

This was an early focus of settlement. Coos Bay was attractive because it could accommodate the small, ocean-going ships of the day. It was in fact, as it still is, the best harbor on the Oregon Coast (Fig. 48). This is not to say that there are no difficulties to navigation. The bar outside the harbor is dangerous and is responsible for many wrecks. When two supply ships appeared off the bar in 1854, the happy settlers went out to meet them in a small boat. The boat overturned and the six occupants drowned.[34] Numerous wrecks and accidents on the Coos Bay bar led to heavier use of the land routes to and from Coos Bay (Fig. 49), either along the beach to the Umpqua River and thence inland to the Willamette Valley or by pack trail to Roseburg on the Oregon-California Trail.

Coos Bay is in the form of an irregular horseshoe (see Fig. 47), looping north from the entrance, then east, and turning around to the south. The general width of the bay varies up to more than a mile. The entrance itself was originally about one mile wide before it was improved by jetties, after which the width was reduced to one-half mile. Various arms of the bay referred to as sloughs or inlets, North Slough, Haynes Slough, Kentuck Slough, reach out from the main body of the bay. Perhaps the most significant of these from the standpoint of early travel was South Slough, which runs south from the vicinity of Barview near the entrance of the bay. South Slough played a very important part in the early travel in the region. The heads of this and other sloughs were settled, beginning in 1854; these farms could only be reached by boat, hence the settlers were called "rowboat pioneers."[35] The level land above the sloughs was fertile and could be extended and protected from salt water by comparatively short dikes across the sloughs. This was done quite early.

In addition to the harbor and the water transport available by the bay and its tributaries, the area offered other attractions to settlers. On the floodplains of the various rivers, especially the Coos and the Coquille, there was level land suitable for cultivation. The coal mines, which were exploited very early, beginning in 1853, attracted many settlers and donation land claims were taken out in these areas even though this did not represent very good agricultural land.

The trails developed in the Coos Bay-Coquille area were related to the shoreline or to settlement. Prior to 1860 there were three important focal points of settlement; Empire, about four miles inland from the entrance to the bay, settled in 1850; the Coal Bank Slough area, two miles southwest of the present city of Coos Bay; and the Marshfield area. A number of donation land claims were entered for the Coal Bank Slough area and an additional number in the vicinity of Coquille, but at that time only one donation land claim was taken out at Marshfield, which later became the city of Coos Bay. Empire was the important port for approximately the first ten years of settlement and was the chief focus of the trails (Fig. 51). About 1860 much of the traffic shifted to Marshfield and to the south along Isthmus Slough and via a portage to the Coquille River and Bandon.

The easiest approach to Coos Bay was from the north (see Trail (A), Fig. 47). As previously mentioned, the Umpqua River provided the easiest route

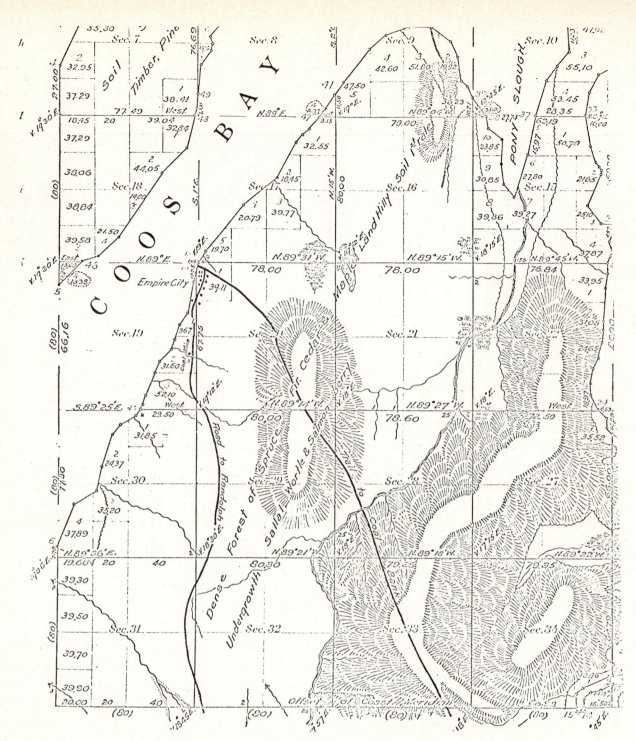

Fig. 51. This portion of Land Office Map T25S R13W (1857) shows the trails from Empire toward Randolph and toward Coal Bank Slough. Subsequent issues of this same township map include trails to Marshfield and North Bend. (Compare Fig. 23.)

from the Willamette Valley or from the Oregon-California Trail to the mid-section of the Oregon Coast. From the Umpqua River southward the trail led along the beach and for many decades this was the only trail or way connecting these two points. In 1854 this route was established officially as a county road from Empire City to Ten Mile Creek and it was considered necessary to put up markers to guide travelers so that they could avoid quicksand.[36] It would appear from the conditions of the beach today that the fears

[56]

Empire City in 1856 (*Harper's New Monthly Magazine,* October, 1856, Vol. XIII).

of quicksand were somewhat exaggerated. This road, long known simply as the Beach Route, continued to be one of the main arteries of travel into and out of Coos Bay until the coming of the Southern Pacific Railroad in 1916. It was not until the 1920s that a surfaced road was constructed into Coos Bay from the north to take the traffic away from the beach.

The approach from the south near the shore was much more difficult (see Trail (B), Fig. 47). The traveler coming along the beach, heading north, as Jedediah Smith was in 1828, had easy going from the Coquille River near Bandon for several miles along the beach or along the Whisky Run terrace less than 100 feet above the beach. The trail along the terrace is outlined on the early maps. Near Five Mile Creek, however, the beach ended and it was necessary to travel over very rough country if one wanted to stay near the coast. On July 4, 1828, Jedediah Smith and his party traveled from the vicinity of Whisky Run along the beach to the end and then traveled over the rough country, "as we were obliged to cross the low hills, as they came in close to the beach, and the beach

Fig. 52. The Cape Arago-Seven Devils area was crossed with great difficulty by Jedediah Smith in 1828 (white line). Later an easier route, the Randolph Trail, led inland. The bad ravines, mentioned by Smith, are clearly shown. (U.S. Geological Survey photo)

being so bad that we could not get along, thicketty and timbered, and some very bad ravenes to cross (Fig. 52)."[37] Smith and his party reached the vicinity of Cape Arago where they camped. On the next day they traveled only one and one-half miles. This was partly because the horses were tired but partly because of the dense vegetation. On July 6th they traveled only two miles. Smith described the trail as "very bad, mirery, and brushy; several horses snagged very bad, passing over fallen hemlock." It was necessary to clear a trail from the ocean shore to the present site of Charleston, after which they ferried across South Slough.

Inland the marine terraces in the Coos Bay area offered many advantages to the early travelers. A series of steps or benches range from a low terrace in the vicinity of Coos Bay (city) and only slightly above

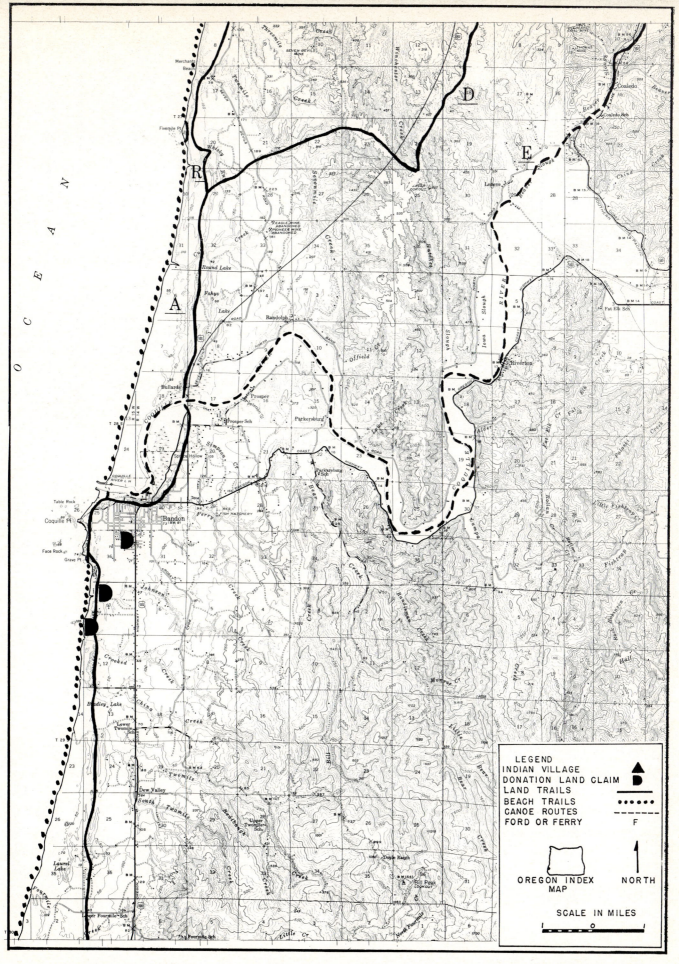

Fig. 50. Trails of the Bandon area. Three routes led from Bandon toward Coos Bay; (A) along the shore, either on the beach or the terrace, passing the old mining camp of Randolph (R); (D), the Empire-Randolph Trail, along the high terraces; (E) the water route on the Coquille River (see Fig. 16). Base map: Bandon and Coquille quadrangles. Land Office maps T27S R14W (1857) and T28S R14W (1857).

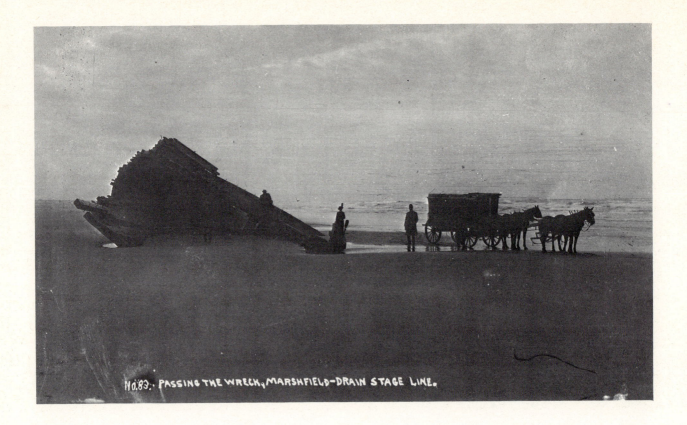
NO.83. PASSING THE WRECK, MARSHFIELD-DRAIN STAGE LINE.

sea level to terraces several hundred feet above sea level.[38] The most important terrace from the standpoint of trails was the 100-foot terrace, also called the Whisky Run terrace from a small stream by this name a few miles north of the Coquille River. This terrace is nearly level on top and covered with sand and gravel, so that it afforded good footing even in the wettest weather. The terrace continues south of Bandon and the records show that it was used more than the beaches. The higher terraces were used inland and especially the 400-foot terrace figured largely in the trail from the vicinity of Whisky Run inland and then northward to connect with Marshfield and Empire (see Figs. 47 and 50).

One inland trail (see Trail (C), Fig. 47) from the south took off near the north end of the beach at Five Mile Creek and crossed the hills and terraces to the east, reaching the southern tip of South Slough. From this point water transportation was available north to Coos Bay and, of course, to various other settlements. This route was not suitable for a party with pack animals.

A branch of the coast trail (see Trail (D), Fig. 50) left the coast at Whisky Run, near the site of the Randolph mining camp (see (R), Fig. 50), trending eastward to the high terraces and then northward to the vicinity of Coos Bay. Near the coalfields on Coal Bank Slough this trail divided, one part going to Empire and the other going to Marshfield. In this area there were several trails connecting the key points; a trail led directly from Empire to the coalfields and another trail led eastward to the North Bend area.

Another route (see (E), Figs. 47 and 50), much used in the early days, made maximum use of water transportation. The traveler approaching the Coos Bay-Coquille area from the south (see Fig. 50), arriving at Bandon, would take passage in a canoe or small boat, travel up the Coquille River to Beaver Slough, up Beaver Slough as far as possible, and then, making a portage across the low divide, again utilize water transportation in Isthmus Slough to Coos Bay. This was a favorite way of transporting freight not only from the south but principally from the trail which reached Isthmus Slough from Roseburg. (The trail

Looking south from Cape Blanco, 1964. (Seufert Col., OHS)

from Roseburg to Coos Bay (see (F), Fig. 50) became important when the railroad reached Roseburg in 1872.) The difficulties encountered in this route were the beaver dams and dense vegetation, which all but met overhead in the narrower parts of the slough. Many descriptions of this journey are available from the 1850s and most of the travelers were very unhappy with the conditions. The improved route, still difficult, was described by Walling in 1884:

> Traffic between the Coquille valley and Coos bay is conducted very peculiarly. Travelers may pass between Coquille City and Marshfield by means of a road, difficult and sometimes nearly impassable; or they may take the celebrated Beaver slough route, by which freight is usually brought into the Coquille region. It is a very peculiar mode of traveling and somewhat beyond ordinary powers of description. Poets have sung the terrors and trials incident to the Beaver slough passage, and careworn passengers have compared the whole thing to the horrors of the African slave ships. Setting out from Myrtle Point, the traveler is ordinarily compelled to walk about a mile and a half when, Providence permitting, he is taken into a small boat and rowed to the *Ceres* or the *Little Annie,* and conveyed to the mouth of Beaver slough, a few miles below Coquille City; here awaits him a long double-ended skiff, manned by two oarsmen, whose business it is to pole the boat up the narrow, still, and tortuous, ditch-like slough for a few miles, when the traveler gets into a wagon and is transported several miles further to the far-famed isthmus railway, where, on a car drawn by a dummy engine, he is brought to Isthmus slough at a point where the water is navigable to the bay and he reaches Marshfield, finishing his journey by steamer, after having experienced the delights of travel on foot, in skiffs, by two different steamers, in a mud-wagon and by train, at an expense of a dollar or two and a day's time.[39]

The Cape Ferrelo Area

Many of Curry County's early settlers and travelers arrived from the south, including Jedediah Smith, first to describe the trails. Therefore the descriptions to follow begin at the California line, in the Cape Ferrelo area, and extend northward to Cape Blanco. The Cape Ferrelo area, extending from the Winchuck River on the south, north to the Pistol River, was one of the most difficult portions of the southern Oregon Coast (Fig. 53). Aside from the first few miles near the California line, the terrain is rugged with many

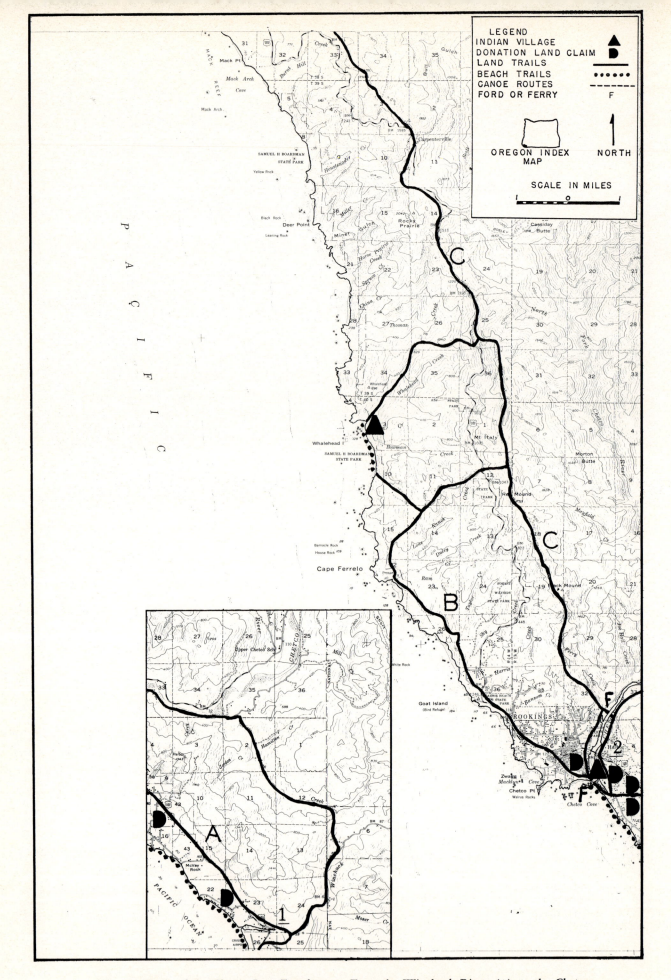

Fig. 53. Trails of the Chetco-Cape Ferrelo area. From the Winchuck River (1) to the Chetco River (2) three routes were used (inset map). North of the Chetco River most of the travel was on the ridge trail, about two miles from the rugged shore. Base map: Cape Ferrelo and Mt. Emily quadrangles. Coast Survey charts T 1227 (1871) (see Fig. 5) and T 1260 (1871), and Land Office maps T39S R14W (1873), T40S R14W (1873), and T41S R13W (1858).

Fig. 54. Whalehead Beach was a definite part of the Coast Trail. Whalehead Point (left) provided some protection from northwest winds and was used as a boat landing. (See Fig. 4.) (Ore. State Highway photo)

small creeks cutting deep canyons in the hills, so that a trail close to the shore was not feasible, either by way of the beaches or immediately above them on the sea cliffs. The vegetation near the shore was nearly all brush or chaparral, the result of burnings by the Indians. Above this and inland a mile or more, there was forest, an easier place to travel.

The first obstacle encountered by the traveler crossing the 42nd Parallel from California was the Winchuck River. Here the trail made a detour inland for a little over one mile where the Winchuck River could readily be forded (see Fig. 9). Then the trail looped back toward the coast and followed along the edge of the foothills at the upper part of the marine terrace.

Jedediah Smith and his party arrived in Oregon from California on June 23, 1828.[40] After camping near the Winchuck River, Smith and his party forded the stream at low tide, probably at some distance from the outlet. Then they "kept along under the mountain," at the upper edge of the marine terrace (see (A) on Fig. 53, inset map) where "many little streams breaks out . . . and makes it a little mirery," which caused some difficulty with the horses. A part of the journey was along the beach, suggesting that they tried first one route and then another. Likely there was an Indian trail along the foot of the hills, leading to a ford located on the Chetco River a few miles above the mouth. The marine terrace, over which they traveled between the Winchuck and Chetco rivers and first settled in the years 1853-1855 as donation land claims, proved to be the best site for settlement on the southern Oregon Coast.

[63]

Fig. 55. This double natural bridge on the Curry County coast near Thomas Creek illustrates the difficulty of travel. No record was found of travel along this section of the coast. (Ore. State Highway photo)

Arriving at the Chetco River, they were unable to ford it because of high tide. The Indian village had been quickly deserted as the party approached and the travelers saw none of the Indians until the following day. The Chetco River was forded near the outlet at low tide and the travelers continued northwestward near the coast (see (B), Fig. 53) for 12 miles on June 25th. Smith and his party probably passed the site of Lone Ranch (see Fig. 53), then turned inland a bit, but returned to the coast at Whalehead Beach (see (4), Figs. 53 and 54). This beach, a little over a mile long, afforded easy travel and also a good camping place near an Indian village. In later years Whalehead Cove was sometimes used as a landing for small boats carrying produce to San Francisco. From this point the trail turned inland again toward the ridge because of the extremely rugged coastline (Fig. 55).

The main trail from the Chetco River northward (Trail (C), Fig. 53) was along the ridge which is about two to three miles inland in most places. The ridge trail offered advantages in that it was mostly in the forest rather than in the brush; there were few or

[64]

Fig. 56. A short trail led over Cape Sebastian as indicated by the white line. A longer trail farther inland was more suited to pack animals. (Ore. State Highway photo)

no streams to cross on the ridge; and it was well used. This was probably the main Indian trail and certainly it was the one mostly used by the settlers. In the north, at least, it corresponds to the position of the old Highway 101 via Carpenterville; to the south it connected to the Chetco River by the upper ford (see Fig. 53). It is undoubtedly the best site for a trail or road in this area and, together with the alternate route via Whalehead, continued in use until road construction began, much of it on the same route, many years later.

Following the period of the donation land claims, which were located mainly on the terrace southeast of the Chetco River, a few homesteads were settled near the ridge trail between the Chetco and Pistol rivers, but this rugged, hilly land was unsuitable for farming, both by climate and terrain, and most of these homesteads failed, to be succeeded by a few large ranches.

On June 26th, the Smith party ascended to the ridge and followed the main trail all the way to the Pistol River (see Figs. 53 and 57). Nearly 60 years later this trail, still the only land link between Ellensburg (Gold Beach) and Brookings, was described by A. G. Walling:

The trail southward from Ellensburg crosses Hunter's creek, a small stream, with a narrow valley, cultivated by a few settlers. The region all about is extremely wild and romantic, both ocean and mountainward. Grazing is much pursued, and upon the "prairies" many sheep may be seen. Between Hunter's creek and Pistol river the trail ascends a very high mountain [Cape San Sebastian, Fig. 56], where a splendid view of the Pacific may be gained. Pistol river is larger than the first mentioned stream, and is fifteen miles by the trail from Rogue river. . . . The Chetco river or creek is crossed by two ferries—Miller's, nearest the mouth, and Smith's, two miles above.[41]

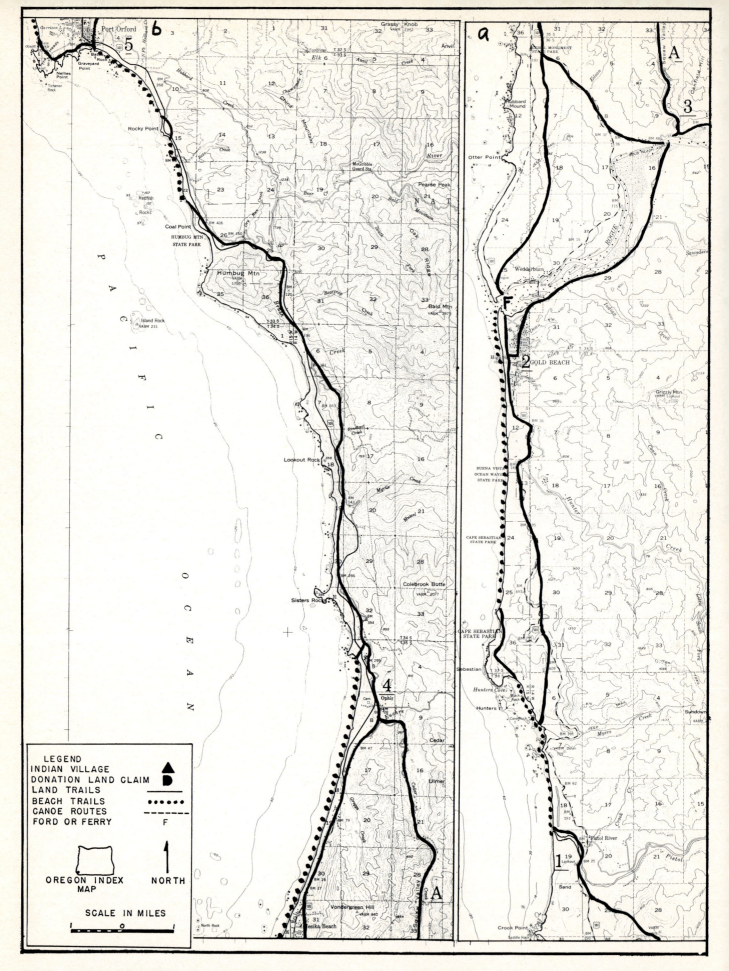

Fig. 57. Trails of the Gold Beach and Port Orford area. North of the Pistol River (1) travel was on the beach, except for headlands, but an alternate trail was available to Gold Beach (2). An easy crossing of the Rogue River, a few miles inland (3), led to the use of an alternate trail (A). North of Ophir (4) the beach was apparently little used, except near Port Orford (5). Base map: Gold Beach (a) and Port Orford (b) quadrangles. Coast Survey charts T1133 (1869) and T 1862 (1888), and Land Office maps T31S R15W (1857), T32S R15W (1857), T33S R14W (1857), T34S R14W (1875), T36S R14W (1857), T36S R15W (1857), T37S R14W (1881), and T38S R14W (1873).

The Gold Beach-Port Orford Area

There were only two settlements of note in this area, one at the mouth of the Rogue River and the other at Port Orford.[42] (Fig. 57.) In both places forts were built by the civilians and soldiers for protection against the Indians. At Ellensburg (Gold Beach) a settlers' fort, Fort Miner, was built on the north side of the Rogue River in open prairie country (no cover for Indians[43]), whereas the settlement was on the south side of the river. The beaches in this area were generally short and unsatisfactory for travel. For this reason the trail in many places was not on the beach and sometimes not very near it.

Jedediah Smith and his party entered this area on June 26th and camped at Pistol River. The next day they moved on to the Rogue River, crossed the following day, and passed Port Orford on July 1st. The beach was followed from the Pistol River as far as Cape Sebastian, which had to be crossed by an Indian trail. After that the party continued on the beach to the Rogue River. Rafts were used to ferry the packs across the narrow entrance to the Rogue River (Fig. 58); the horses had to swim and 12 of them were drowned in the operation.

After settlements were established on the lower Rogue River, a number of alternate trails were marked out (see Fig. 57). Perhaps the most important alternate coast route in this vicinity led northward from the upper crossing, about five miles above the mouth of the Rogue River (Fig. 59). Here was a fairly easy crossing of the river at the head of tide and the first riffle, as one ascends the stream. The trail continued up Squaw Valley, over a low divide to Cedar Creek, following the route later used by old Highway 101. This was one of the many inland routes preferred by some travelers, even if the streams were not navigable by canoes. A shortcut from the Squaw Creek ford led northwestward and joined the coastal trail, three miles north of the Rogue River.

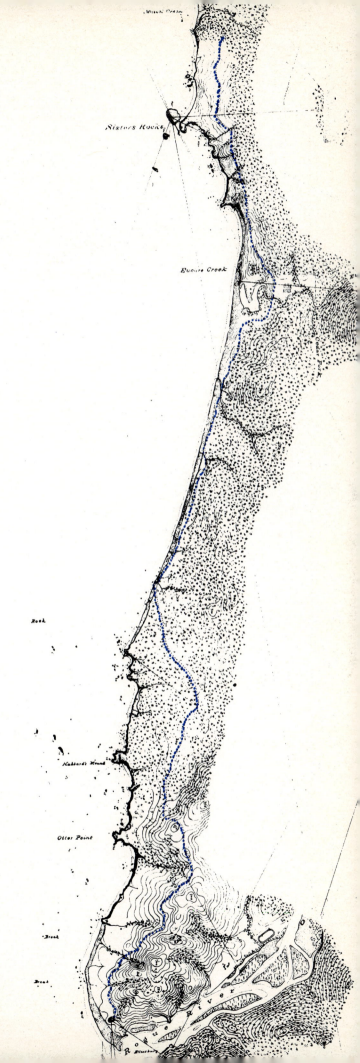

Fig. 58. A portion of the old chart of the Rogue River and vicinity, showing the coast trail to the north. (U.S. Coast Survey Chart No. 759, OHS, 1888)

Fig. 59 (above). The upper crossing of the Rogue River (F) led to an inland trail (white line). The beach and the terrace above it were apparently little used. Otter Point, left center. *Fig. 60* (below): Landslides on the Oregon Coast were difficult to cross with pack animals. The prehistoric slide south of Humbug Mountain, is still active. (Univ. of California Engineers photos)

Fig. 61. The northbound traveler left the beach south of Humbug Mountain and followed Brush Creek to the north. (See Fig. 57) (Ore. State Highway photo)

No important trail led inland directly up the Rogue River. The trail indicated on the map (see (3), Fig. 57) played out at a short distance because of the narrow gorge. There is no room on the margins of the river for land travel and the cliffs are too steep to climb. Instead, trails led over the ridges to Agness on the Illinois-Rogue confluence and other trails reached the upper Rogue River by somewhat roundabout routes, one via Port Orford.

North of the Rogue River, the Smith party continued along the beach as tide would permit, otherwise traveled over the hills. In many cases high tide prevented the use of the beach and forced the party into somewhat difficult going on the terraces or hills. This brought them to Euchre Creek, the present site of Ophir. North of Euchre Creek (see Fig. 57) the trail continued near the coast, mostly on the terraces and low foothills, rarely on the beaches except only the long beach immediately south of Port Orford. On June 29th the Smith party made only five miles, to Mussel Creek. Although there are short beaches in this stretch, there are also rocky points, such as Sisters Rocks, and

Fig. 62. The highway north of Humbug Mountain follows almost exactly the route of the old Coast Trail. (Ore. State Highway photo)

it was difficult to climb down the cliffs to reach the beaches and climb out again. This is an area of frequent landslides (Fig. 60), including prehistoric ones, with many wet, miry places which made it difficult for the horses. On June 30th they traveled one mile to Lookout Rock and then six miles more along Brush Creek to the coast. It is likely that the Smith party camped near the outlet of Brush Creek which is now the site of Humbug State Park. Brush Creek runs around the east and north side of Humbug Mountain (Fig. 61), and the route was well-marked by an Indian trail which crossed the creek frequently to find the best terrain. North of Humbug Mountain the trail continued along the edge of the terrace to Port Orford (Fig. 62).

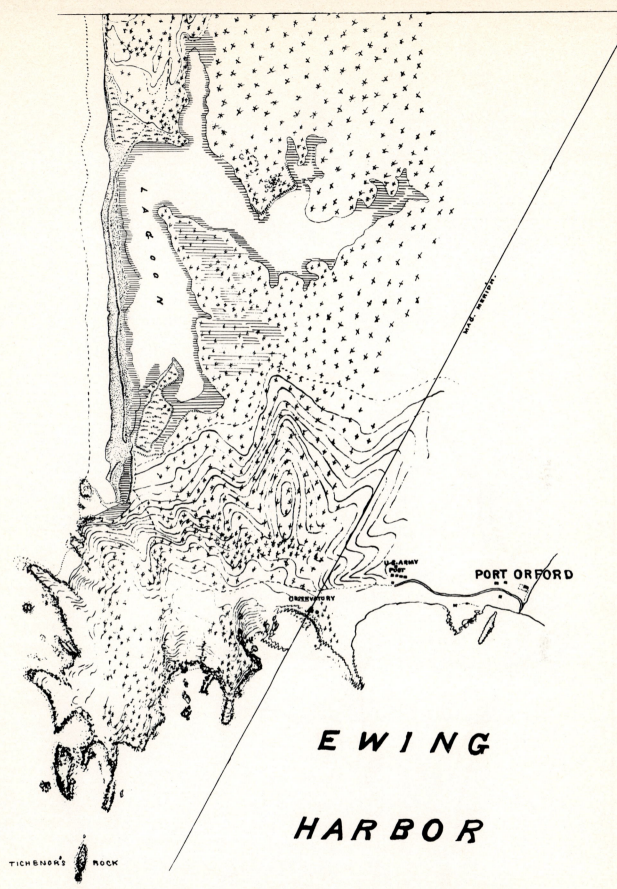

Fig. 64. Old chart of Port Orford, showing the trail (line of dashes) northward along the coast from the Army post. (U.S. Coast Survey, No. 764, OHS, 1851)

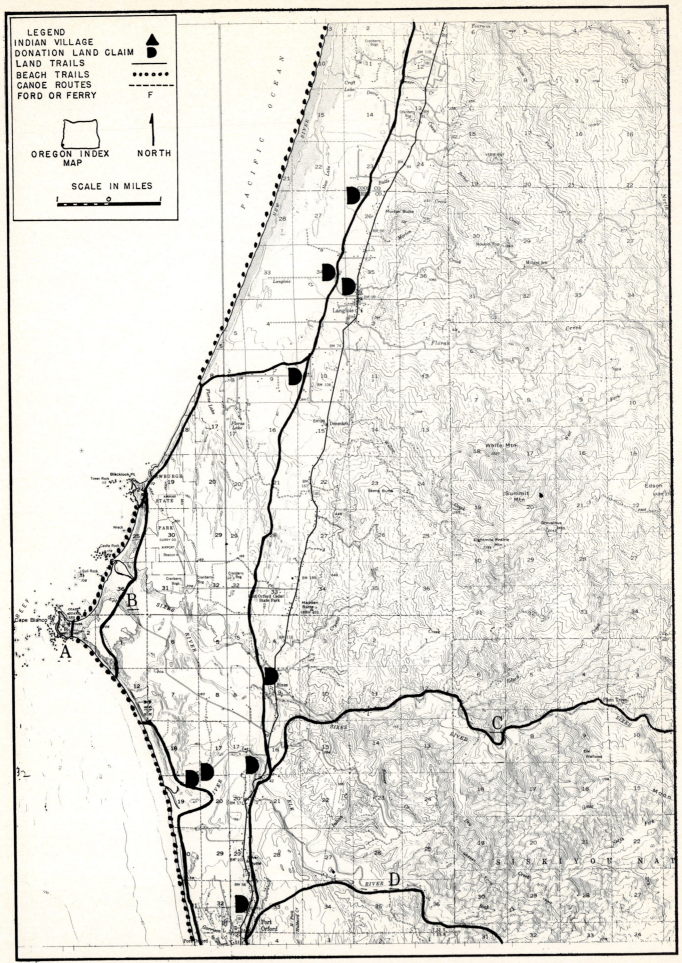

Fig. 63. Trails of the Cape Blanco area. Two short trails, (A) and (B), by-passed Cape Blanco (see Fig. 21). The inland trail followed the wide terrace on which were several donation land claims. The trails east were temporary and led to the placer mines near the headwaters of the Sixes River (C) and the Elk River (D). Base map: Cape Bnaco and Langlois quadrangles. Coast Survey Chart T 1133 (1869), and Land Office maps T31S R13W (1872), T31S R15W (1857), T32S R14W (1857), and T32S R15W (1857).

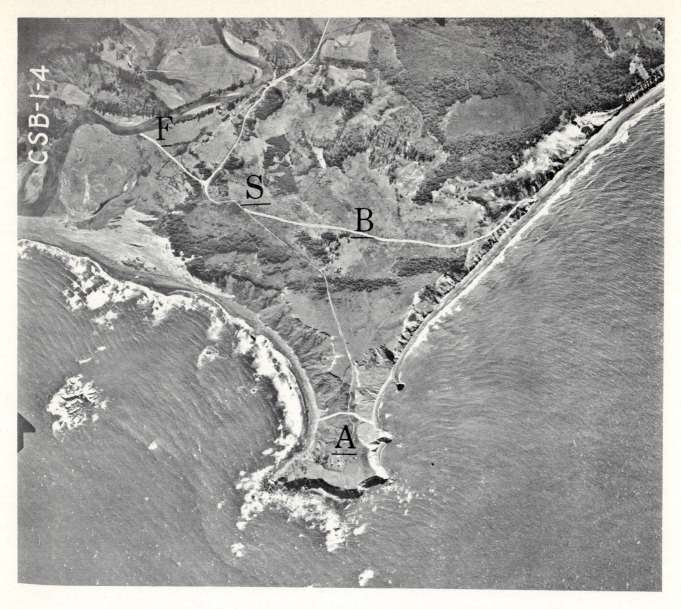

Fig. 65. Vertical airphoto of the Cape Blanco area. One short, steep trail (A) crossed the cape near the point. Another (B), more suitable for pack animals, crossed the terrace farther to the east, passing the settlement (S), and continued to an easy crossing of the Sixes River (F). (U.S. Forest Service photo)

THE CAPE BLANCO AREA

Cape Blanco, a prominent headland, is the extreme western part of a broad terrace (Fig. 63), from two to five miles wide. This terrace attracted settlers early, mostly because of the gold in the beach sands and terrace gravels. Many who came to mine stayed to farm; three donation land claims were located near Langlois, one on the Sixes River where the inland trail crossed the river, three on the lower Elk River, and one immediately north of Port Orford. In this area there were some settlements related to mining. The best sites for placer mining were along the edge of the foothills, in other words, the upper part of the terrace. Here the terrace gravels contained a good deal of gold which could be successfully washed. Attempts at mining the gold-bearing sands on the beaches were not so successful.

The favorite location for a farm was on the east margin of the terrace next to the foothills and this meant that a trail was developed in this location. Most of these farms were dairy farms in the early days and their produce was generally shipped to San Francisco. Later some of these farms changed their character and one of them, on the lower Sixes River, became a sheep ranch.

The Cape Blanco marine terrace is a continuation of the Whisky Run terrace mentioned previously. The streams, especially the Sixes and Elk rivers, have cut fairly broad valleys into the terrace and the floodplains of these streams afforded some agricultural land. Here and there are lakes, Garrison Lake on the south, Floras Lake in the middle section, and New Lake farther north. Parallel to the beach is New River which is an outlet for Floras Lake and afforded an opportunity for the early travelers to use boats for some distance very near the beach.

The terrace area was burned over frequently and was by no means completely reforested when the early travelers arrived. Jedediah Smith describes the vegetation as small pine and, although he traveled along the edge of the terrace at times, he makes no mention of difficult vegetation The earliest main trail, from Brush Creek to Port Orford, was near the beach; but north of Port Orford it led inland. A detour was necessary to ford Elk River, carrying the trail about a mile inland and then returning it to the beach area near the outlet of Elk River. Cape Blanco (Figs. 64 and 65) was crossed by a short trail which led across the base of the cape to the lower Sixes River crossing, one-half mile from the sea. From that point the traveler ascended to the terrace and followed it to a point beyond Floras Lake. The beach immediately to the south and north of Blacklock Point is bordered by a very steep cliff and is not usable even at mid-tide (see Fig. 7). North of Floras Lake this main trail divided, one section turning eastward to connect with the inland trail, the other continuing up the beach to Bandon and the Coquille River.

The inland trail (see Fig. 63) left Port Orford to the east of Garrison Lake and continued in a generally northward direction, more or less paralleling the present Highway 101, in some places being almost a mile to the west of the highway. The location of this route is well authenticated from the early charts, the Coast Survey, and from the maps of the Surveyor General. Early maps show two trails branching off to the east from Port Orford, one following up the Elk River and the other up the Sixes River. These trails are marked on the early maps "to the mines," and carried the traveler to the gold mines on the various tributaries of the South Fork of the Coquille River. The first miners to work this area came in by sea to Port Orford.

Roosevelt Highway photos, probably of the 1920s and early 1930s. OHS Collections. (pp. 75-76).

From Trails to Roads

TRAILS were gradually widened and improved but nearly three-quarters of a century passed before many of them were converted to all-weather roads. Eventually the Coast Trail was replaced by Highway 101. This long delay in road building may be explained in several ways. In many stretches of the coast the beach afforded a very good road, tide and weather permitting. Tide and weather would not wait, but the early travelers were not usually in a hurry; they could and did wait for tide and weather. Road building was delayed also by the very nature of the steep terrain and the character of the thick soils. Landslides are a natural phenomenon on the coast and the construction of even a narrow road accelerates them. But the greatest handicap to road building was the thin population and the lack of resources. Not until 1932 could it be said that the Coast Highway was completed.[44]

As roads were built many of the old trails disappeared. Some were obliterated by road construction; others vanished under the rapid growth of vegetation; erosion, especially landslides, destroyed some sections. In western Oregon a trail is a temporary thing unless it is used continuously. Some parts of the old trails are kept up today for recreational purposes in the state parks, especially on the headlands.[45] The Ecola Park Trail over Tillamook Head is almost the same route as the one followed by William Clark in 1806. The trail over Cape Lookout, now greatly improved, was used by John Frost in 1841. In other places faint remnants of the trails remain, somewhat confused with the recent tramplings of men and animals.

ROOSEVELT HIGHWAY- CURRY CO- ORE. NO.124.

BEN JONES MEMORIAL BRIDGE OVER ROCKY CREEK - OREGON COAST HIGHWAY.

CAPE TUNNEL- MANZANITA TO CANNON BEACH, OREGON CO

ALSEA BAY BRIDGE - 3028 FEET LONG - OREGON COAST HIGHWAY, OREGON.

Footnotes

1. Daniel Lee and J. H. Frost, *Ten Years in Oregon* (New York, 1844), 85.
2. A. R. McLeod, "Journal of a Hunting Expedition South of the Umpqua . . . September, 1826," in *Peter Skene Ogden's Snake Country Journal 1826-1827*, K. G. Davies, ed. (Hudson's Bay Record Society, XXIII, London, 1961), lviii-lxi, 174-215.
3. Harrison C. Dale, ed., *The Ashley-Smith Explorations and the Discovery of a Central Route to the Pacific, 1822-1829* (rev. ed., Glendale, California, 1941), 265-80.
4. Lewis A. McArthur, "The Pacific Coast Survey of 1849 and 1850," *Oregon Historical Quarterly*, XVI (Sept., 1915), 264.
5. Ada M. Orcutt, *Tillamook: Land of Many Waters* (Portland, 1951), 47.
6. Oscar Winslow Hoop, "History of Fort Hoskins, 1856-1865," *OHQ*, XXX (Dec., 1929), 349-50.
7. McArthur, "Pacific Coast Survey," *OHQ*, XVI: 255.
8. Joel V. Berreman, *Tribal Distribution in Oregon* (Memoirs of the American Anthropological Association No. 47, Menasha, Wisc., 1937), 1-40. See also Orvil Dodge, *Pioneer History of Coos and Curry Counties, Or.* (Salem, 1898), 104-13.
9. Dale, *Ashley-Smith Explorations*, 255.
10. David Douglas, "Journal of David Douglas. . . , 1824-'25-'26-'27," *OHQ*, VI (March, 1905), 78. See also Samuel N. Dicken, *et al.*, "Some Recent Physical Changes of the Oregon Coast" (limited distribution, Dept. of Geography, University of Oregon, Eugene, 1961), p. 14. (Nonr-2771 (04), Project NR 388-062, U. of O. and Office of Naval Research, U. S. Navy Department.)
11. Emil R. Peterson and Alfred Powers, *A Century of Coos and Curry* (Portland, 1952), 84-85.
12. Peterson and Powers, *Century of Coos and Curry*, 484.
13. A. G. Walling, *History of Southern Oregon* (Portland, 1884), 471, 473.
14. Warren N. Vaughn, "Journal, 1851-1854," Oregon Historical Society Ms. 213, pp. 10-45. (Hereafter Vaughn, "Journal.")
15. Charles Stevens, "Letters of Charles Stevens (1854)," E. Ruth Rockwood, ed., *OHQ*, XXXVIII (March, 1937), 81.
16. John H. Frost, "Journal of John H. Frost, 1840-43," Nellie B. Pipes, ed., *OHQ*, XXXV (June, 1934), 139.
17. Reuben G. Thwaites, ed., *Original Journals of the Lewis and Clark Expedition of 1804-1806* (New York, 1905), III: 320-30; Lewis A. McArthur, *Oregon Geographic Names* (3rd ed., Portland, 1952), 601.
18. Frost, "Journal," *OHQ*, XXXV: 236.
19. Vaughn, "Journal," pp. 11-12.
20. S. J. Cotton, *Stories of Nehalem* (Chicago, 1915), 64.
21. Vaughn, "Journal," p. 43.
22. Vaughn, "Journal," p. 71.
23. Frost, "Journal," *OHQ*, XXXV: 235-61.
24. Vaughn, "Journal," pp. 58-59.
25. Vaughn, "Journal," p. 40.
26. David Fagan, *History of Benton County, Oregon* (Portland, 1885), 335.
27. Gunter Barth, ed., *All Quiet on the Yamhill: The Civil War in Oregon; The Journal of Royal A. Bensell* (Eugene, 1959), 140.
28. Bensell, *All Quiet*, loc. cit.
29. McLeod, "Journal," op. cit., 151-73.
30. Bensell, *All Quiet*, 141-50; McLeod, "Journal," op. cit., 163.
31. Verne Bright, "Randolph: Ghost Gold Town of the Oregon Beaches," *OHQ*, LVIII (Dec., 1957), 293-306; Bensell, *All Quiet*, 140.
32. Frances Fuller Victor, *The Early Indian Wars of Oregon* (Salem, 1894), 390-96, 405-407, 414-15, 418-19.
33. See Stephen D. Beckham, "Lonely Outpost: The Army's Ft. Umpqua," *OHQ*, LXX (Sept., 1969).
34. Letter from P. B. Marple, *Weekly* (Portland) *Oregonian*, March 25, 1854, p. 2, col. 4.
35. Charlotte L. Mahaffy, *Coos River Echoes: A Story of the Coos River Valley* (Portland, 1965), 65.
36. Peterson and Powers, *Century of Coos and Curry*, 480.
37. Dale, *Ashley-Smith Explorations*, 271.
38. Ewart M. Baldwin, *Geology of Oregon* (2nd ed., Eugene, 1964), 31.
39. Walling, *History of Southern Oregon*, 488.
40. Dale, *Ashley-Smith Explorations*, 264-70.
41. Walling, *History of Southern Oregon*, 481.
42. Peterson and Powers, *Century of Coos and Curry*, 95.
43. See McArthur, *Oregon Geographic Names*.
44. Leslie M. Scott, "Oregon Coast Highway," *OHQ*, XXXIII (Sept., 1932), 268-70.
45. Some of these modern trails are shown on the recent maps of the U.S. Geological Survey; and also in *100 Oregon Hiking Trails*, by Don and Roberta Lowe (Portland, 1969).